The First Queen Elizabeth

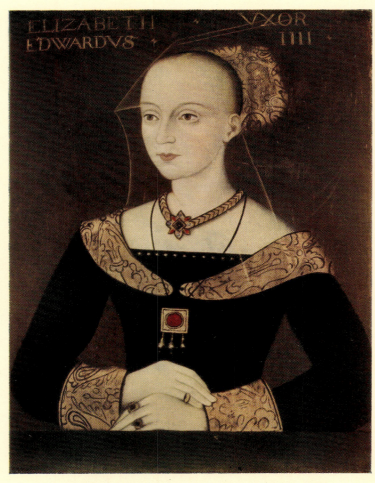

ELIZABETH WOODVILLE, *circa* 1465

(QUEENS' COLLEGE, CAMBRIDGE)

The First Queen Elizabeth

by

KATHARINE DAVIES

LOVAT DICKSON LIMITED
PUBLISHERS
LONDON

First Published 1937

LOVAT DICKSON LIMITED 38 BEDFORD STREET LONDON
AND ST MARTIN'S HOUSE BOND STREET TORONTO

SET AND PRINTED IN GREAT BRITAIN BY
STEPHEN AUSTIN & SONS LIMITED HERTFORD
PAPER SUPPLIED BY SPALDING & HODGE LIMITED
BOUND BY G. &. J. KITCAT LIMITED
SET IN MONOTYPE BASKERVILLE

PREFACE

TO write a life of Elizabeth Woodville is difficult, mainly because there are few of those personal memorials so necessary to the appreciation of character. The chief events of her life are chronicled; her two marriages, her coronation, the birth of her children, the death of her husbands, the tragic events which altered her apparently brilliant destiny to one of the deepest tragedy. But the intimate details which, had she lived only fifty years later, would have been abundantly preserved, have not been recorded. How easy it is to arrive at an idea of the character and appearance of Anne Boleyn, for instance, from letters, sayings, and vivid details of her daily life. But it is quite otherwise with Elizabeth. The descriptions of her which exist were written after her death by men who had not seen her: the intimate touches are lost. From her portraits, few in number, we can deduce that she had brown eyes and golden hair, that she was slender, and that she preserved her figure even after she had borne twelve children, as can be seen from her portrait in the royal window at Canterbury Cathedral, done about the year 1483.

'Man is wise, virtuous, and human, or silly, vain, and wicked, in comparison with his contemporaries. He must be estimated not by a standard of morality erected several centuries after his death, but by the standard of the age and country in which he lived.' [1] Elizabeth Woodville has been judged too harshly. She is not a sufficiently important figure for historians to have spent much time in weighing her merits and demerits, and she has been summarily dismissed as a vain, ambitious, grasping, and capricious woman, in whom it is impossible to find any qualities worth praising. It would be idle to deny that once she found herself Queen of England she did all in her power to advance her family, and that the consequent jealousy of the rival party at court caused the disasters which finally overwhelmed her and so many of her relations. But it is difficult to see what other faults can be laid to her charge. She was a good wife and mother, a loving daughter and sister, a woman of unimpeachable virtue which even her enemies never attempted to slander. In one of the most bloodthirsty periods of English history, the court of Elizabeth and Edward was urbane and refined.

Daughter of a knight, widow of a nobleman, wife of a king, she lived to be persecuted by Richard III, to see her sons murdered and her father and two of her brothers executed; but she lived to see her daughter Queen of England, and the healing of the long and bloody feud between the Houses of York and Lancaster. She is the ancestress of every reigning sovereign since Henry VII.

The name of Woodville is spelt in a variety of ways. William of Worcester spells it Wydvile and

[1] Nicholas.

PREFACE

Wydevile on two successive lines, and Widville elsewhere; Sandford spells it Widevile and Wodevile; it appears as Widville on Elizabeth's tomb, and as Wydville or Wydeville in contemporary documents. As I have mainly used modern spelling throughout my book, I have chosen the modern spelling for Elizabeth's family name, but I do not think that it was ever spelt Woodville in her time.

ACKNOWLEDGMENTS

I wish to acknowledge the kindness of the President and Fellows of Queens' College, Cambridge, in allowing the portrait of Elizabeth Woodville which forms the frontispiece to be reproduced.

I have also to thank the President of Queens' for his courtesy in personally showing me the portrait and the parts of the College which were in existence in Elizabeth's time.

I am also most grateful to Mr. George Smith for allowing me to quote from his book, *The Coronation of Elizabeth Wydeville*; and to Miss Babington, Hon. Steward and Treasurer of Friends of Canterbury Cathedral, for permission to quote from the Tenth Annual Report.

Miss Carola Oman and Miss Helen Ashton have taken a kindly interest in the book and given me valuable assistance.

K. N. D.

CONTENTS

ILLUSTRATIONS

CHAPTER I
ENGLAND IN ELIZABETH'S GIRLHOOD

'Out of monuments, names, words, proverbs, traditions, private records and evidences, fragments of stories, passages of books, and the like, we do save and recover somewhat from the deluge of time.'   *Bacon*

B

ENGLAND IN ELIZABETH'S GIRLHOOD

TO many people there is only one Queen
Elizabeth and she, of course, is Elizabeth
Tudor, that tremendous figure who gave her name
to an age and cast her spell over history. She completely overshadows the two Elizabeths who were
queens before her, partly by her invincible personality, and partly because she was a queen
regnant, whereas they were only consorts. Yet
her grandmother, Elizabeth of York, the last
Plantagenet to wear the crown, and her great-
grandmother, Elizabeth Woodville, the first com-
moner to wear the crown, both played their part
in English history; and the life of the first Queen
Elizabeth, the subject of this book, was so eventful
that she deserves to be better remembered than
she is.

Some may not have forgotten the old tradition
that Elizabeth, the beautiful widow of a Lancastrian
nobleman, won the heart of the handsome, pleasure-
loving Yorkist monarch, Edward IV, when he
caught sight of her beneath a tree, in the forest
where he was hunting. Elizabeth appealed for the
restoration of her husband's confiscated lands, and
won not only her suit, but the King's heart as well.
Some may even remember that she was the mother
of two boys generally known as the Princes in the
Tower, but few know any more of her 'strange,
eventful history'.

The marriage of Edward IV and Elizabeth Woodville is one of the most romantic episodes in English history. A young prince, scarcely established on an uneasy throne, chose to hazard everything in order to marry one of his subjects—a woman whose only dowry was her beauty and her virtue, and whose rank was far beneath his own. It was a dangerous thing to do, but Edward did it, and what is more, he never regretted it. Within the limits of his wayward and dissolute nature he was devoted to Elizabeth, and her influence over him lasted till the end of his life.

It is difficult now to realise the astonishment and dismay which this love-match caused in an age when the only motive for matrimony was material gain; and if this was true of people in general, it always had been true of royal marriages—the only difference was that kings married for the good of the realm, whereas their subjects married for their own good.

The crown was not won for the house of York in a single battle, but after five years of alternate victory and defeat; nor was it kept without a struggle. It was a matter of vital importance to strengthen the new dynasty with the most advantageous alliance which could be secured. This was not easy, for Henry VI was still alive, and the heads of the ruling houses of Europe were cautious; but the Earl of Warwick, the richest and most powerful man in England, the man who made Edward king, busied himself with negotiations, while Edward rode about the country showing his magnificent person to his admiring subjects. Three years passed, and when at length it appeared that the house of York was safely established on the throne, and that England was recovering from her disasters, the neighbouring monarchs became willing and even anxious to secure the alliance which they had mistrusted. But it was too late. Edward had made his own choice. He was the first king of England who married for love and his queen was the first queen who was not of royal blood.

Unconsciously, perhaps, by his marriage Edward typified the new spirit of freedom which was beginning to pervade an era of confusion and transition. In the fourteenth century, the age of Chaucer, Gower, Langland, and Wycliffe, the age which saw the removal of many restrictions on the freedom of the individual, and especially the poor individual, the age which saw the dawning of the power of Parliament, a new spirit had been abroad; and the old spirit of chivalry and service was still far from spent. But the fifteenth century was like dead water between two tides. 'The morning gleam of the Renaissance in England' had faded ; the fine austere spirit of the Middle Ages was dying or dead. The old tide was ebbing; the new tide had been checked, largely owing to the internal dissension which racked the land.

The century opened with a new dynasty when Henry Bolingbroke, the son of John of Gaunt, and the first king of the house of Lancaster, took the crown from his cousin, Richard II. His reign was troubled with rebellion, and when his son, Henry V, came to the throne he sought to divert attention from the weakness of his father's claim by renewing the old war with France. His victories revived the glories of Edward III's time, but during the long minority of his son, Henry VI, who succeeded as an infant, all these conquests were lost. Joan of Arc kindled the spirit of patriotism in the hearts of her countrymen and the English were almost driven out of France. In the effort to pursue the war at all costs affairs at home were neglected, and by the time Henry VI was old enough to rule himself, the country was in a dangerous state. Only a very strong man could have maintained order; but the young king was gentle and pious, interested in learning, and quite out of tune with the ruthless spirit of the time; his one desire was for peace, and especially peace with France. To this end he married Margaret of Anjou, which was a very unpopular move, for by the marriage contract two of the few remaining provinces in France were given back to her father, the Duke of Anjou. The king fell completely under her influence and it was Margaret who ruled the country; but she cared nothing for England or for the welfare of the people. For eight years there was no heir and many looked to Richard, Duke of York, the king's cousin and the next in succession to the throne, as the one hope of reform.

When, at length, a Prince of Wales was born it was too late to stem the tide of rebellion, and war broke out between the two houses of Lancaster and York. It was not at first the intention of either the

Duke of York or of his chief supporter, the Earl of Warwick, to depose Henry: all they sought was better government. But as time went on and first one side had the upper hand and then the other, York, in a moment of victory, pressed his claim to the crown; Parliament would not depose Henry, but it agreed to set aside the Prince of Wales, and to accept York as the Heir Apparent. This Margaret could not brook. She rallied her forces, which defeated York and slew him at Wakefield; and when she also defeated Warwick at the second battle of St Albans it seemed as if nothing could stop her from a complete victory. But she was so hated by the citizens of London that, rather than see her once more in power, they hastened to proclaim Edward, Earl of March, the eldest son of the Duke of York, as the first king of a new dynasty.

Young though he was—he was only nineteen years of age—Edward IV had fought in more than one battle and had recently himself won an important victory. He was very tall and handsome, and he inspired an enthusiasm among his followers which Henry never did. Edward was a leader, whereas Henry was only a figure-head. But he came to the throne at a time when the whole country was in a state of the wildest disorder. Every great land-owner kept his own band of retainers, sometimes numbering thousands, men who had fought in the French wars and were used to deeds of violence; and every noble thought more of his own wealth and importance than of his loyalty to the crown. This love of wealth for its own sake was a striking feature

7

THE FIRST QUEEN ELIZABETH

of the national character at the time; men sought
by every means in their power to add to their
possessions. The simplest way to do this was by
marriage, and there never was a time when the
outlook on marriage was so sordid; people of standing did not marry for love, but for what they could
get; children were bought and sold in their cradles.
A man laid out so much money and purchased the
hand of a child: he hoped to get his capital back
with interest when the youthful bride or bridegroom
brought estates into the family. It was a custom
which had become universal, and nobody saw anything disgraceful in it. A man expected sympathy
when he wrote: 'For very need, I was forced to sell
a little daughter I have for much less than I
should.' People not only trafficked in their own
children's marriages, but they bought up wardships
in order to profit by selling the hand of the ward.
Soon after Edward came to the throne, he rewarded
a Devonshire lady named Joanna Dynham, who
had helped him to escape from England in a
moment of defeat, with the wardship and marriage
of a young tenant-in-chief of the Crown.

Almost the only chance which a woman had to
marry for love was if she became a widow; but if
her second husband happened to be of inferior
station and fortune to herself, then she was considered to have brought disgrace upon her whole
family. If a royal lady did such a thing, the consequences were very serious.

Yet these scandals did occur, and in the reign of
Henry VI there were two notorious cases. Katharine

8

of France, the widow of Henry V, married a Welsh-
man named Owen Tudor, who—though he boasted
the usual fantastic Welsh pedigree in which, as has
been said, the name of Noah occurs somewhere
about the middle, and which in this case included
Cadwallader, the legendary last king of the Britons
—was nevertheless only a knight. Hall, that entertaining chronicler of the sixteenth century,
describes the marriage thus :

'This woman, after the death of King Henry the
fifth, her husband, being young and lusty, following
more her own appetite than friendly council, and
regarding more her private affection than her open
honour, took to husband privily a goodly gentleman and a beautiful person, garnished with many
goodly gifts, both of nature and of grace, called
Owen Tudor.'

As will be seen later on, this marriage, which was
considered disgraceful at the time, proved of extraordinary importance in the end ; but this was not
the only *mésalliance* which Hall has reason to
deplore. He writes further:

'The Duchess of Bedford, sister to Lewis, Earl
of Saint Pol, minding also to marry rather for
pleasure than for honour, without council of her
friends, married a lusty knight, Sir Richard Woodville, to the great displeasure of her uncle, the
Bishop of Thérouanne; but they could not remedy
it, for the chance was cast and passed.'

The marriages of these two sisters-in-law did not
go unpunished, although Katharine suffered the
more severely. She managed to conceal her rash act

for several years, but when it was at length found out her husband was imprisoned, her children were taken from her, and she herself was obliged to seek refuge in a convent. The Duchess of Bedford was less unfortunate, though she was fined a thousand pounds, a vast sum in those days; but it was not long before the young couple were back at court, and apparently in high favour.

Jacquetta, Duchess of Bedford, was of royal birth, a daughter of the princely house of Luxembourg, and as the widow of Henry VI's uncle John, Duke of Bedford, she was a lady of some importance; indeed, in 1437, about the time when her first child, Elizabeth, was born, the death of two queens altered her position considerably. It was a year of sinister omens and is summarised in the following manner by one of the chroniclers: 'This year died Queen Katharine, the which was King Harry the fifth's wife. Also this year fell down a tower of London Bridge, with two arches and all that stood thereupon. Also this same year died Queen Jane, King Harry the fourth's wife. Also this same year died all the lions that were in the Tower of London.' It is not known how the fate of these unfortunate animals affected the Woodville family, but on the death of the two queens, Sir Richard found himself the husband of the first lady in England, and his prospects seemed bright indeed. In 1441 he was chosen as champion of England to fight against a Spanish champion in a tournament which was held before the king at Smithfield.

In 1445 the Duchess and her husband were among those who sailed to France to bring home the King's bride, Margaret of Anjou, and the deference paid to the Duchess's rank is shown by the fact that a large ship called the Swallow was assigned to her, whereas Sir Richard and his followers had to travel in a smaller boat. When the beautiful and dangerous Margaret arrived in London, the citizens paid her the sweet compliment of wearing daisies in their hats. Better would it have been for the whole country if she had never landed.

Nevertheless she was a good friend to the Duchess of Bedford; they were connected by marriage, and Margaret was probably glad to find a fellow countrywoman among the strangers who now surrounded her.

Sir Richard was created Baron Rivers in 1449, and in the following year he received the superlative honour of being made a Knight of the Garter. He was entrusted with the organisation of a military expedition to Aquitaine, which, however, came to nothing owing to lack of money, and afterwards he spent some years in command of the garrison at Calais.

Nothing is known of Elizabeth's childhood, though it may be supposed to have been largely passed at Grafton [1] in Northamptonshire, the ancestral home of the Woodvilles; but there can be no doubt that the family life of the Woodvilles was happy: they were devoted to each other, and they clung together throughout their lives in a way which afterwards brought down on them the envious hatred of their enemies. Elizabeth certainly had no lonely

---

[1] See Appendix 1—'Grafton Manor and the Woodville family.'

childhood, for the cradle at Grafton was never empty. After her birth, twelve children followed in rapid succession, and were named Anthony, John, Richard, Margaret, Anne, Jacquetta, Joan, Edward, Lionel, Catherine, Mary, and Martha. Out of this long list of names those of Anthony and Lionel alone stand out on their own merits. Anthony is a figure who faintly foreshadows the soldier-scholars of the next century; like Surrey, Wyatt, and Sidney, he used the pen as well as the lance and sword. Lionel entered the Church, and became Bishop of Salisbury and Chancellor of Oxford University.

It is possible that Elizabeth was for a time lady-in-waiting to Margaret of Anjou. Sir Thomas More says: 'This Elizabeth, being in service with Queen Margaret, wife to King Henry VI, was married to one John Grey, whom King Henry made knight at the last battle of Saint Alban's, but little while he enjoyed his knighthood, for at the same battle he was slain.' [1]

The name of Domina Isabella Grey (Isabella being written in Latin for Elizabeth) occurs in 1445, and again in 1453, amongst the ladies attending on Margaret, but it seems most likely that the first mention refers to the mother of John Grey who was also called Elizabeth. However, there is a possibility that Elizabeth Woodville was already married in 1453, when she was sixteen years old, and she was undoubtedly married by 1456, because in that year certain manors were enfeoffed by her father-in-law to provide an income for his son on his marriage.

[1] See Appendix 2—The Letters of Sir Hugh Johns.

John Grey was the eldest son and heir of Lord Ferrers of Groby, owner of Bradgate in Leicestershire, the future birthplace of Lady Jane Grey.

The married life of the young couple must have been clouded by the unhappy state of England at the time, as hostilities between the Duke of York and Henry VI broke out at the first battle of St Albans in 1445, and lasted intermittently till the second battle of St Albans in 1461, when Henry was deposed, and Edward IV was proclaimed king. It was an anxious moment for the families of Grey and Woodville, who were both staunch Lancastrians. Elizabeth was left a widow with two young children; Lord Rivers and his sons were fighting for a dethroned and fugitive monarch; the Duchess of Bedford was trembling for the fate of her dowry, and for the future of her unmarried daughters. They could not foresee that the winter of their discontent would soon be made glorious summer by this sun of York.

CHAPTER II

EDWARD, EARL OF MARCH

'There sprang a Rose in Rouen that spread to England.'
Old Song

EDWARD, EARL OF MARCH

THIS Earl of March, who now, as Edward IV,
wore the crown of England, was born in Rouen
on 28th April, 1442. He was doubly descended
from that tremendous progenitor Edward III, for
besides the royal lineage of his father, the Duke of
York, his mother was Cecily Neville, the youngest
of the children of Ralph, first Earl of Westmoreland,
by his second wife, Joan Beaufort, daughter of John
of Gaunt.

From his mother Edward is said to have inherited
his great personal beauty, which was afterwards
described so enthusiastically by the chroniclers:
'This King Edward was a man of goodly personages,
of stature high, and exceeding all other in countenance, well favoured and comely, of eyes quick and
pleasant, broad-breasted and well set.' Philip de
Commines, who had seen him, said that he was the
handsomest man of his time. In the eighteenth
century, when his coffin was opened, his skeleton
was found to measure six foot and three inches, and
his long brown hair was still in perfect preservation.

His character was complex. Beneath an outward
appearance of such charm and affability as to win
the hearts of all who came in contact with him, he
hid a treacherous and cruel disposition. He was
courageous in battle and a brilliant soldier, yet in
private life he was indolent and voluptuous. He was
not a scholar, but he was fond of books; he collected

a valuable library, and became the patron of
Caxton. St George's Chapel, at Windsor, is the
chief monument to his love of building, which took
rather the form of modernising the old palaces which
were in use when he came to the throne, and of
bringing them up to the requirements in comfort
of a luxurious court. His love of dress was notorious
and he was always magnificently attired.

At the time of his birth in Rouen, his father was
Regent of France. Henry VI was still only a boy,
and as the Duke of York was then heir presumptive
to the throne, Edward was a child of some importance. He was only two years old when his father
arranged for him the first of a series of ambitious
marriages, none of which was to take place. The
bride chosen was Madeleine, daughter of Charles VII
of France; she was then a promising young woman
of six months. York would really have preferred the
princess's elder sister Jeanne, who was already
thirteen years of age, because he was anxious for his
son to raise up heirs as soon as possible; but the
King of France would not agree. Probably he
realised that Edward might never come to the
throne, and so he did not want to waste a valuable
daughter who might any day now make a more use-
ful marriage. While these matrimonial negotiations
were proceeding, Margaret of Anjou passed through
Normandy on her way to England: she was entertained by the Duke of York; and perhaps the first
seeds of her subsequent hatred for him were sown
when she found that he was seeking the King of
France's daughter for his son's bride, while the King

of England was only marrying the daughter of the Count of Anjou.

The next event in the life of the young Earl was his establishment at his father's castle at Ludlow, in Shropshire, with his brother Edmund, Earl of Rutland, who was born a year later than himself. This was shortly after 1445, when the Duke of York's term of office in France expired. Edward was placed under the control of a gentleman named Sir Richard Croft, whose wife, referred to as 'the Lady Governess', was a near kinswoman of Cecily Neville's; but as the young Earl of March was only a baby still, his French nurse, Anne of Caux, at first looked after him. This woman seems to have been the faithful servant of the family for many years, for not only did Edward, when he became king, pay her a pension of twenty pounds a year, but his brother Richard of Gloucester, who was the youngest but one of the fourteen children of the Duke and Duchess of York, continued the grant, when by steps far less innocent than those which she had guided, he came at last to the throne.

Sir Richard Croft was a stern disciplinarian and his rule occasioned the young princes, some years later, to write to their father the following letter:—

'We thank your noblesse and good fatherhood of our green gowns now late sent us to our great comfort; beseeching your good lordship to remember our porteux (breviaries) and that we might have some fine bonnets sent unto us by the next sure messenger, for necessity so requireth. Over this, right noble lord and father, please it your Highness to wit that we have charged your servant, William Smyth, bearer of these, for to declare unto your nobility certain things on our behalf, namely concerning and touching the odious rule and demeaning of Richard Croft and his brother. Wherefore we beseech your gracious lordship and full noble fatherhood to hear him in exposition of the same, and to his relation to give full faith and credence.'

Here seem foreshadowed two characteristics in Edward's personality which were afterwards very conspicuous: his love of dress and the great fascination which he exercised over those around him; young though he was he could at any rate influence the soft-hearted William Smith to side with him against 'the odious rule'. Perhaps the hard-hearted Sir Richard sometimes punished the boys by putting them on bread and water, and there seems a suggestion at the end of the following letter that although the boys are dutifully getting on with their work, yet a friend in the kitchen would not come amiss:

'And it please your Highness to know of our welfare, at the making of this letter we were in good health of bodies, thanked be God, beseeching your good gracious fatherhood of your daily blessing. And where ye command us by your said letters to attend specially to our learning in our young age that should cause us to grow to honour and worship in our old age, please it your Highness to wit that we have attended our learning sith we come hither, and shall hereafter; by the which we trust to God your gracious lordship and good fatherhood shall be pleased. Also we beseech your good lordship that it may please you to send us Harry Lovedeyne, groom of your kitchen, whose service is to us right agreeable; and we will send you John Boyes to wait on your lordship.'

Perhaps in later life Edward did not look back with any disagreeable feelings on the years of his boyhood at Ludlow, as he had his own two sons brought up there.

When Edward was eleven years old, the birth of a son to Henry and Margaret, on 13th October, 1453, considerably altered his prospects: as the King and Queen had been married for eight years without having any children, the unexpected appearance of a Prince of Wales must have been a great disappointment to the Duke of York, and probably he was not averse to fostering the rumours which flew about that the child was not really the son of his father. Henry is reported to have said that the prince 'must be the son of the Holy Ghost', but as his mind had unfortunately begun to fail, no importance was attached to this statement. But the scene, when the Queen presented the long wished-for baby to his father, was pathetic for Henry only cast down his eyes and would not look at his son.

Edward remained quietly at Ludlow till he was about thirteen; but the times were too troubled for much book-learning and he appears to have been present at the first battle of St Albans in 1455, when his father and his cousin, the Earl of Warwick, won a great victory and took the king prisoner for the first time. It was after this battle that Warwick was made Captain of Calais, the most important military post in the realm; and here, five years later, the young Edward met his future father-in-law in not very auspicious circumstances.

Hostilities had broken out again. Henry won the battle of Ludlow, and the Duke of York fled to Ireland. Warwick retired to Calais, where he knew he was safe, and Edward went with him. It was in vain that Henry gave the Captaincy to the young Duke of Somerset whose father had been Captain. Somerset was greeted with cannon-balls when he sailed into the port, and he was obliged to retire to Guines and send for reinforcements. Upon this Lord Rivers was commanded to assemble some ships at Sandwich, and to go to his assistance. It would have been a great feather in Rivers' cap if he could have dislodged the Earl and captured Calais, but things turned out differently. Warwick had his spies in Kent, a county which was Yorkist in sympathy, and he soon heard of what was going on at Sandwich.

He organized a raid by night and ignominiously captured Lord Rivers, the Duchess of Bedford, and their son Sir Anthony, as they were asleep in their beds, and at four o'clock on a cold January morning carried them back across the 'narrow sea', and the whole fleet with them,

Pained indeed must Lord Rivers have been when he arrived at the port which he had hoped to capture, but more pained still when he came into the presence of the three Earls, Warwick, his father Salisbury, and March.

It seems likely that his feelings got the better of him, and that he imprudently accused the three Lords of treachery, The scene, which is described in two of the Paston letters, laughably recalls school prefects sitting in judgment on a cheeky junior, or three old Colonels in a club speaking their minds to some upstart socialist who has dared to express his political opinions:—

'As for tidings, I send some off hand written to you and others, how Lord Rivers, Sir Anthony his son, and others have won Calais by a feeble assault made at Sandwich by Dynham, Squire, with the number of eight hundred men on Tuesday between four and five o'clock in the morning. . . . My Lord Rivers was brought to Calais and before the Lords with eight score torches, and there my Lord of Salisbury rated him, calling him knave's son, that he should be so rude to call him and these other Lords traitors, for they shall be found the King's true liegemen when he should be found a traitor, etc. And my Lord of Warwick rated him and said that his father was but a squire and brought up with Henry the Fifth, and sithen himself made by marriage, and also made lord, and that it was not his part to have such language of lords, being the king's blood. And my Lord of March rated him in likewise. And Sir Anthony was rated for his language of all three lords in like wise.'

Soon after this undignified scene Warwick landed in England and was triumphantly received in London. The months which followed were fatal alike to Henry and the Duke of York, but triumphant

23

for Edward. Henry was defeated and taken prisoner at the battle of Northampton: a battle at
which the eighteen-year-old Edward actually commanded a part of the army. The Duke of York
chose this moment to make a spectacular bid for
the throne, and although he failed to realize his
ambition, he did so far succeed that Parliament
agreed to accept him as Heir Apparent instead of the
Prince of Wales. Naturally this was the signal for
Margaret to rally her adherents in defence of the
rights of her son, and scarcely a month after his
triumph York and his second son, the Earl of
Rutland, a boy of sixteen, were killed at Wakefield;
the head of the aspirant to the throne of England
was ironically crowned with a paper crown and
placed over the gates of York.

Inspired by her victory, Margaret proceeded to
gather an army of wild and lawless men on the
Border, to whom she promised unlimited plunder,
and as she marched south these men committed
fearful excesses, 'spoiling Abbeys and houses of
religion and churches . . . as they had been paynims
or Saracens or no Christian men,' so that the fear
of them spread through the whole country. For the
second time in the Wars of the Roses St Albans was
the scene of a great battle, and here, strangely
enough, the king and queen were on opposite sides,
for Henry was still virtually a prisoner in the hands
of Warwick. Margaret was victorious, and when
Warwick had fled, Henry was found 'under a great
oak tree laughing to see the discomfiture of the
army'. It seemed now as though nothing could

stop Margaret from a complete triumph, but while she paused to let her soldiers lay waste the town and abbey of St Albans, the citizens of London determined that they would not allow her within the walls. At this juncture the Duchess of Bedford earned the gratitude of the City for, with two other ladies, she went to the Queen and interceded with her 'for to be benevolent and owe goodwill to the city'.

While these negotiations were proceeding, Warwick was on his way to join Edward, who was at Shrewsbury when the news of the disasters reached him. He might well have been dismayed, and indeed he must have felt the loss of his father and brother most keenly, for his family affection was one of his best qualities; he was spurred on to revenge, and hastily gathering an army he won a brilliant victory at Mortimers Cross. He then met the Earl of Warwick 'on Cotswold', and they rode straight to London.

Up till now Warwick had been faithful to Henry, though always opposed to Margaret; but he saw that the time had come when he must either fly the kingdom or else make one last desperate bid for success by attempting to place Edward on the throne. The ease with which this was achieved was astonishing. It was not only that London welcomed Warwick as the man who could save them from Margaret's dreaded Northernmen, but they saw in Edward a young man of the most inspiring presence. Parliament was not sitting, so the only thing to do was to present Edward to the people

25

and lay before them those claims which his father had made before him. Four times, in four different places, this was done, and at St Paul's, and in Westminster Hall, and in the Abbey, Edward himself addressed the crowds. Nothing could have been happier than this personal appeal on his part: it was something quite new, which seemed to promise friendship between the king and his people. The blood of the Mortimers in his veins must have endowed him with the musical voice and the natural oratory which characterises the Welsh, and the impression which he made was overwhelming. When the people were asked whether they would have Edward instead of Henry they cried:'Yea! Yea! King Edward!' The whole city rang with the praise of this fortunate young man.

Edward's reign began on 4th March, 1461; but if London was willing to have a Yorkist monarchy the whole of England was not so minded, and the very day after his accession preparations were made to continue the war. Margaret and Henry had withdrawn to the North, and by the end of the month Edward was in Yorkshire and the terrible battle of Towton was fought on Palm Sunday, in the most inclement weather. No quarter was given. 'This field was sore fought. For there were slain on both parts 33,000 men and all the season it snowed.' Margaret and Henry fled into Scotland, and Edward entered York in triumph, through those very gates over which the heads of his father and brother still stood. After celebrating Easter, he turned southward and made his way slowly through his kingdom, meting out punishment or pardon, till he came to Stony Stratford in Northamptonshire, near to the home of Lord Rivers at Grafton. The whole future of the Woodville family depended on the outcome of this visit.

There is unfortunately no direct evidence of any meeting between Elizabeth Woodville and Edward before their marriage, so that it can only be surmised that it was the sight of her beauty which influenced him to pardon her father and brothers. If there is any truth in the old tradition that Edward first saw Elizabeth when he was hunting in the forest of Whittlebury, near Grafton, then it may well have been now that the scene occurred; but whether the meeting took place at this time or not, when the king left Stony Stratford two days later he had 'pardoned and remitted and forgiven unto Richard Woodville, Lord Rivers, all manner of offences and trespasses of him done against us', and before long 'the king affectionately considering the state and benefit of Jacquetta, Duchess of Bedford', paid her the annual amount of her dowry 'three hundred and thirty three marks four shillings and a third of a farthing' and even wrote several letters to his Treasurer about the matter.

CHAPTER III
EDWARD MARRIES ELIZABETH

'And so, privilie in a morning, he married her at Grafton, where he first phantasied her visage.'

Hall's Chronicle

CHAPTER III

EDWARD MARRIES ELIZABETH

EDWARD went back to London from Stony
Stratford to prepare for his coronation, which
was celebrated on 28th June, 1461, in a manner
quite out of keeping with the empty exchequer;
for although in time Edward became extremely
wealthy from the confiscated property of Henry and
the Lancastrian nobles, during the first months of
his reign he was obliged to borrow money where he
could. He meant to give the citizens of London
a sight worth seeing, and the keeper of the Wardrobe received £1,000 in ready money—a sum equal
to ten times that amount to-day—for the expenses
which would be incurred.

'The Rich Crown of King Edward' (Edward the
Confessor), which was kept at the Treasury in a
'little coffin of leather bound with iron and locken
with divers locks and keys', was placed on his head
by the two Archbishops, after which the lords and
ladies, and a delegation of the citizens of London,
sat down to the Coronation Banquet in Westminster
Hall. Among the Knights of the Bath created were
the King's two brothers, George and Richard; a
little later George was made Duke of Clarence, and
Richard Duke of Gloucester, and both received the
Garter.

But after these joyful scenes were over, the business of straightening out the tangled affairs of the
kingdom demanded attention; yet when Parliament

met and the Chancellor, Bishop Neville, had addressed it on the text 'Amend your ways and your doings', no legislation of any importance was introduced beyond the attainting of Henry and Margaret and a number of Lancastrian nobles.

The question of Edward's marriage was naturally a matter of great importance to his adherents, for it was not yet clear how the establishment of the new dynasty of York would be received abroad, and an alliance with one of his powerful neighbours would greatly strengthen Edward's position. Scotland was frankly on the side of Henry; Charles VII of France had died within a month of the Coronation, and the attitude of his crafty son, Louis XI, was not yet known; Philip of Burgundy alone was friendly. Consequently the first plans for Edward's marriage lay in the direction of Burgundy, and an embassy was sent in the autumn of 1461 to ask for the hand of Philip's niece, Catherine of Bourbon. Philip, however, was a cautious prince; Henry and his son were still alive: he preferred to wait and see whether Edward was firmly seated on the throne before he so far committed himself.

In an attempt to come to terms with Scotland, Warwick then suggested a match with Mary of Gueldres, the mother of the young King James II; but she was many years older than Edward, and as the political situation between the two countries was too confused to be quickly settled, the negotiations were only of a tentative nature and came to nothing.

If Mary of Gueldres was too old, the next lady was

EDWARD IV

(ALBURY PARK)

too young. In 1464 Henry the Impotent of Castile offered the hand of his sister Isabella, aged thirteen, to the twenty-two year old Edward; but by this time Warwick was firmly convinced that an alliance with France was essential, and he was asking for the sister of Louis XI's queen, while Edward had secretly made up his mind to marry a lady of no political importance. Years later, when Edward was dead, and Isabella had long been the Queen of Castile and the wife of Ferdinand of Aragon, she still remembered the slight which she had received and she told the ambassador of Richard III that she was 'turned in her heart from England in time past for the unkindness the which she took against the king last deceased for his refusing of her and taking to his wife a widow of England'.

In passing, it is amusing to notice that Hall, whose comments on matrimony are always entertaining, supposed Isabella to be only six or seven years old 'at which time King Edward had fully accomplished twenty-three years and more. The treaty of which marriage, although it be not *un*possible, yet for the causes aforesaid it seemeth a little unlikely. BUT' (and here the capital letters which form the first word of every paragraph in Hall's Chronicle seem most significant) 'now consider the old proverb to be true that sayeth: that marriage is destiny. For during the time that the Earl of Warwick was thus in France concluding a marriage for King Edward, the King, being on hunting in the forest of Wychwood beside Stony Stratford, came for his recreation to the Manor of Grafton, where the Duchess of

Bedford sojourned, then wife to Sir Richard Woodville, Lord Rivers, on whom was attending a
daughter of hers called Dame Elizabeth Gray,
widow of Sir John Gray, Knight, slain at the last
battle of St Albans, by the power of King Edward.
This widow having a suit to the King . . . found
such grace in the King's eyes that he not only
favoured her suit, but much more fantasied her
person. . . . For she was a woman . . . of such
beauty and favour that with her sober demeanour,
lovely looking and feminine smiling (neither too
wanton nor too humble) beside her tongue so
eloquent and her wit so pregnant, . . . she allured
and made subject to her the heart of so great a
king.

'After that King Edward had well considered all
the lineaments of her body and the wise and
womanly demeanour that he saw in her, he determined first to attempt if he might provoke her to be
his sovereign lady promising her many gifts and
fair rewards, affirming further that if she would
thereunto condescend, she might so fortune of his
paramour and concubine, to be changed to his wife
and lawful bedfellow, which demand she so wisely
and with so covert speech answered and repugned,
affirming that, as she was for his honour far unable
to be his spouse and bedfellow, so for her own poor
honesty, she was too good to be either his concubine
or sovereign lady: that where he was a little before
heated with the dart of Cupido, he was now all on
a hot burning fire what for the confidence that he
had in her perfect deliberation, he determined with

himself clearly to marry with her, after that asking counsel of them which he knew neither would nor once durst impugn his concluded purpose.'

Hall's description of the courtship is interesting, because he tells us that the king was 'on hunting in the forest of Wychwood',[1] which goes to confirm the old tradition that Edward and Elizabeth first met under a great tree, where she had stationed herself with her two little boys, in the hope of making her suit to the king. This tree was for long called by the country people of Northamptonshire, 'The Queen's Oak.'

The scene is so charming in imagination that it would be a pity to set it aside altogether, even though it is now the fashion to discredit all such picturesque traditions, so that we are not to believe that Shakespeare poached Sir Henry Lacy's deer, or that Clarence was drowned in a butt of Malmsey wine.

The royal hunt comes trotting through the forest, with the jingle of harness and the eager whimpering of the hounds: (it would doubtless be more dramatic to picture them as in full cry after a stag: but even 'the face that launched a thousand ships' could hardly induce an enthusiastic follower to turn aside from a hot run.) In the midst of his courtiers rides the King, looking like a young god, and all unaware that he is about to be struck by 'the dart of Cupido'. And when he has seen Elizabeth under the tree, he might say with Orsino:

[1] Actually the tradition refers to Whittlebury Forest in Northamptonshire.

'That instant was I turned into a hart;
And my desires, like fell and cruel hounds,
E'er since pursue me.'

A more prosaic version of the story would be that the King, who is known to have been at Stony Stratford twice before his marriage, met Elizabeth by secret appointment under the oak tree, once or even several times, during the autumn following his coronation. As the Duchess of Bedford and Lord Rivers were about the Court again and apparently in favour, soon after they were pardoned, it is obvious that Elizabeth could be there too, and that many opportunities would occur for her and the King to meet in other places than beneath the oak tree.

In Shakespeare's *King Henry VI Part 3* (Act III, Scene 2) Elizabeth comes to Westminster Palace to plead for the restoration of her lands; Gloucester and Clarence are present to supply the humour by their innuendoes; Edward suffers a *coup de foudre*, makes his dishonourable proposals, and then repents and offers marriage, all in the space of ten minutes. Yet in spite of its absurdity the scene is not without its poetry: the early Shakespeare is clumsy but undoubtedly shows the powers which he later brought to fulfilment.[1]

After Lady Gray has stated her case, the King makes veiled suggestions of an amorous nature.

Lady Grey Why stops my Lord? Shall I not hear my task?

[1] See also other passages from Shakespeare quoted in Appendix 6, p. 244.

King Edward An easy task; 'tis but to love a king.

Lady G. That's soon performed because I am a subject.

King E. Why, then, thy husband's lands I freely give thee.

Lady G. I take my leave with many thousand thanks.

Gloster (aside to Clarence) The match is made; she seals it with a curtsey.

King E. But stay thee,—'tis the fruits of love I mean.

Lady G. The fruits of love I mean, my loving liege.

King E. Ay, but, I fear me, in another sense.
What love, think'st thou, I sue so much to get?

Lady G. My love till death, my humble thanks, my prayers;
That love which virtue begs and virtue grants.

King E. No, by my troth, I did not mean such love.

Lady Grey is annoyed at the King's 'merry inclination' and Gloster says:

The widow likes him not, she knits her brows.

Clarence (aside to Gloster) He is the bluntest wooer in Christendom.

After which the King relents and proposes marriage more bluntly than ever: Lady Grey mistakes his meaning:

Lady G. I know I am too mean to be your queen,
And yet too good to be your concubine.

King E. You cavil, widow: I did mean, my queen.

Lady G. 'Twill grieve your Grace my sons should call you father.

King E. No more than when my daughters call thee mother.

Thou art a widow, and thou hast children;
And, by God's mother, I, being a bachelor,
Have other some: why, 'tis a happy thing
To be the father unto many sons.
Answer no more, for thou shalt be my queen.

Which command Lady Grey obeys: nor does she open her mouth again during the rest of the scene, not even to bid good-bye when the King, still bluntly, dismisses her with the passionate words 'Widow, go you along'.[1]

This scene would seem to be based on More's description of the wooing, which is worth quoting at length:

'After, when King Edward was King, and the Earl of Warwick being on his embassage, this poor lady made her suit to the King to be restored to such small lands as her husband had given her in jointure; whom when the King beheld, and heard her speak, as she was both fair and of good favour, moderate of stature, well-made, and very wise; he not alone pitied her, but also waxed enamoured on her, and taking her secretly aside, began to enter into talking more familiarly, whose appetite when she perceived, she virtuously denied him, but that

---

[1] *History of Richard the Third*. Sir Thomas More.

she did so wisely, and that with so good manner, and words so well set, that she rather kindled his desire than quenched it. And finally, after many a meeting and much wooing, and many great promises, she well perceived the King's affection towards her so greatly increased, that she durst somewhat the more boldly to say her mind, as to him whose heart she perceived more fervently set than to fall off for a word. And in conclusion she showed him plain, that as she thought herself too simple to be his wife, so she thought herself too good to be his concubine. The King much marvelling at her constancy, as he that had not been before elsewhere so stiffly said nay, so much esteemed her continence and chastity, that he set her virtue instead of possession and riches; and thus taking counsel of his own desire, determined in haste to marry her.

'And after that he was thus appointed, and had between then twain assured her, then asked he counsel of his secret friends, and that in such manner, that they might easily perceive that it booted them not to say nay.'

It is certain that the Earl of Warwick was not one of the 'secret friends' who were consulted in such a one-sided manner; he was busily negotiating the French marriage, and the King took care to keep him in the dark.

But there was one whom Edward felt obliged to tell about his daring project, and that was his mother. Up till now he had been a dutiful son; indeed she was said 'to rule the King as she pleases'; but the rest of More's description shows

that in this instance she could not get her own
way:

'Notwithstanding, the Duchess of York, his
mother, was so sore moved therewith, that she dis-
suaded that marriage as much as she possible might,
alleging that it was his honour, profit, and surety, to
marry in some noble progeny out of his realm, whereupon depended great strength to his estate by that
affinity, and great possibility of increase of his
dominions. And that he could not well otherwise do,
considering the Earl of Warwick had so far forth
entered into the matter already, which was not like to
take it well if all his voyage were in such wise frustrate,
and his appointment deluded. And she said further,
"that it was not princely to marry his own subject,
no greater occasion leading thereunto; no possessions nor other commodity depending thereupon,
but only as a rich man would marry his maiden
only for a little wanton dotage upon her person.
In which marriage many men commend more the
maiden's fortune than the man's wisdom; and yet
she said that there was more honesty than honour
in this marriage; forasmuch as there is not between
a merchant and his maid so great a difference, as
between a King and his subject, a great prince and
a poor widow. In whose person, although there was
nothing to be misliked, yet was there, said she,
nothing so excellent but that it might be found in
divers other that were more meet," quoth she, "for
your estate, yea and maidens also, the only widow-
hood of Dame Elizabeth Grey (although she were
in all other points and things convenient for you)

should suffice, as I think, to refrain you from her
marriage, since it is an unfitting thing, and a great
blemish to the sacred majesty of a prince, that
ought as near to approach priesthood in cleanness,
as he doth in dignity, to be defiled with bigamy in
his first marriage." The King made his mother an
answer, part in earnest, and part in play merrily,
as he that knew himself out of her rule: and albeit
he would that she should take it well, yet was he
at a point in his own mind, took she it well or
otherwise. Howbeit, somewhat to satisfy her, he
said, that albeit marriage being a spiritual thing,
ought rather to be made for the respect of God;
where his grace inclineth the parties ought to
incline to love together (as he trusted it was in his
case) rather than for the regard of any temporal
advantage; yet nevertheless he deemed this
marriage well considered not to be unprofitable,
for he reckoned the amity of no earthly nation to
be so necessary for him as the friendship of his own,
which he thought likely to bear him so much the
more hearty favour, in that he disdained not to
marry with one of his own land: and yet if outward
alliance were thought so requisite, he would find
the means to enter thereunto much better by other
of his kin, where all parties could be contented,
than to marry himself, wherein he should never
haply love, and for the possibility of possessions
lose the fruit and pleasure of this that he had
already. For small pleasure taketh a man of all
that ever he hath beside, if he be wived against his
appetite, and "I doubt not", quoth he, "but there

be, as you say, others that be in every point comparable with her; and therefore I let not them that like them to marry them, no more is it reason that it mislike any man that I marry where it liketh me. And I am sure, that my cousin of Warwick neither loveth me so little, to grudge at that that I love, nor is so unreasonable, to look that I should in choice of a wife rather be ruled by his eye than by my own, as though I were a ward that were bound to marry by the appointment of a guardian. I would not be a King with that condition, to forbear mine own liberty in choice of mine own marriage. As for possibility of more inheritance by new affinity in strange lands, is oft the occasion of more trouble than profit. And we have already title by that means, as sufficeth to so much, as sufficeth to get and keep well in one man's days. That she is a widow and hath already children. By God his blessed Lady, I am a bachelor and have some too, and each of us hath a proof, that neither of us is like to be barren. And therefore, madame, I pray you be content, I trust to God she shall bring forth a young prince that shall please you. And as for the bigamy, let the Bishop hardly lay it to my charge when I come to take orders, for I understand it is forbidden a priest, but I never knew that it was forbidden a prince."

'The Duchess with these words nothing appeased, and seeing the King so set on, that she could not pluck him back, so highly she disdained that, under pretence of her duty towards God, she devised to disturb this marriage, and rather to help that he should marry one Dame Elizabeth Lucy, whom the King not long before had gotten with child, wherefore the King's mother objected openly against this marriage. As it were in discharge of her conscience, that the King was sure to Dame Elizabeth Lucy, and her husband before God, by reason of which words such obstacle was made in that matter, that either the bishop durst not, or the King would not proceed to the solemnisation of the marriage, till his fame were clearly purged, and the truth well and openly testified. Whereupon Dame Elizabeth Lucy was sent for, and albeit she was by the King's mother and many others put in good comfort that she was ensured to the King, yet when she was solemnly sworn to say the truth, she confessed that she was never ensured. Howbeit, she said, his Grace spake such loving words to her, that she verily hoped that he would have married her, and if such kind words had not been, she would never have showed such kindness to him, to let him so kindly get her with child. This examination solemnly taken, it was clearly proved that there was no impediment to let the King to marry; wherefore he shortly after, at Grafton, beside Stony Stratford, married the Lady Elizabeth Grey, very privately, which was his enemy's wife, and had prayed heartily for his loss, in the which God loved her better, than to grant her her boon, for then had she not been his wife.'

Edward's behaviour in 'so kindly ' getting Dame Elizabeth Lucy with child is disagreeable; his boast about his 'daughters', though as a jest in the style of the period it rings true, may have been an exaggeration. He is only known to have had two illegitimate children at the time, both by Dame Elizabeth Lucy. These were Arthur and Elizabeth Plantagenet, both born before his marriage, and their existence, of which Elizabeth Woodville must have known, probably made her all the more cautious of putting much confidence in Edward's promises.

Nevertheless, one conclusion can be drawn from the vague accounts of the courtship, namely that Elizabeth Woodville was a virtuous woman. To be the mistress of a King was not considered a great dishonour in those days, and the material advantages to herself and her family would have been considerable. When Edward first professed his love, she cannot have supposed that, by refusing him, she would induce him to make her his queen, and even later on the arguments which the Duchess of York produced against the marriage would be in Elizabeth's mind as well. At a time when girls married so young and were often mothers at sixteen or seventeen, a woman of twenty-seven was considered of very mature years, and this was probably Elizabeth's age in 1464.

If we are to suppose that Edward was making love to her at various times during the first years of his reign, when, headstrong though he was, he could hardly have dared to defy Warwick and risk such a marriage, then we must conclude that Elizabeth thought more of her honour than of the advantages which she might reap from the connection. Although Louis XI, when the marriage was finally announced, thought fit to tell the Milanese ambassador that Edward had married a widow by whom he had already two children, no word was ever breathed in England against her character.

But what a moment it must have been for Elizabeth Woodville when she realized the future that lay before her: that not the proud Duchess of York, nor the great family of Neville, nor the King of France himself, weighed with Edward against his love. Writers have suggested that it was the clever scheming of the Duchess of Bedford which brought about the match, and the ignorant people of the time attributed it to sorcery. Sorcery it was, but of a different kind, which bewitched the King, and although men might seek everywhere for the reason of this amazing marriage, actually it was the simplest in the world. Edward loved, and Edward was a king: a king who meant to have his own way.

The reason for Warwick's determination to bring about a French marriage was his deep-seated conviction that by such a move Louis XI would be obliged to give up helping Margaret. Margaret had not ceased to intrigue with France since she and Henry had been driven out of England into Scotland, after the Battle of Towton, and she was not unsuccessful in her effort. She went in person to France, and she secured a loan and a small number of ships and men from the inscrutable Louis, though he declined to do more. But Margaret made a great mistake in thinking that the English would be pleased at her landing in England with an army of Frenchmen, the very people they hated most. Consequently when she appeared in Northumberland in 1462 very few came to her assistance, and although she at first captured the great castles of Bamborough, Dunstanborough, and Alnwick, when the Earl of Warwick and Edward himself came north to resist her, she was driven out of the kingdom. Taking her son with her, and parting from her husband, whom she was never to see again, she fled, completely destitute, to her father's court in Lorraine, where she lived for the next seven years.

The Lancastrian cause now seemed hopeless; but Henry made one last effort in the spring of 1464. Once more Edward prepared to go north, and on the last day of April he arrived at Stony Stratford; the two previous days had been spent at St Albans, and probably communications had passed between him and Elizabeth, who was then at Grafton. All his life he was a man who regarded omens, and now he had made up his mind to be married on May Day.

'In such pastime, in very secret manner, upon the first day of May, King Edward espoused Elizabeth, late wife of Sir John Gray, Knight, which spousals were solemnised early in the morning, at a town named Grafton, near unto Stoney Stratford; at which marriage was no one present but the spouse, the spousess, the Duchess of Bedford, her mother, the priest, two gentlewomen and a young man to help the priest sing. After which spousals ended he went to bed and so tarried there upon three or four hours, and after departed and rode again to Stony Stratford, and came in manner as though he had been hunting. And within a day or two after he sent to Grafton, to the Lord Rivers, father unto his wife, showing to him that he would come and lodge with him a certain season, where he was received with all honour, and so tarried there by the space of four days. In which season she nightly to his bed was brought, in so secret manner that almost none but her mother was council.' [1]

[1] Fabyan's Chronicle, p. 654.

CHAPTER IV

'HONOURS, RICHES, MARRIAGE BLESSING'

'The golden round,
Which fate and metaphysical aid doth seem
To have thee crown'd withal.'

Macbeth

E

'HONOURS, RICHES, MARRIAGE BLESSING'

THE last effort of the Lancastrians in Northumberland ended in disaster before Edward got there. Warwick's brother, John Neville, Lord Montague, won the battle of Hedgeley Moor on 25th April, and the battle of Hexham on 8th May. Henry escaped, leaving only his hat behind, a bycocket 'garnished with two crowns and fret with pearls and rich stones', which was presented to Edward when he arrived at Pontefract a fortnight after his wedding.

Although the worst of the rising was over, the great castles of Alnwick, Dunstanborough, and Bamborough still held out; Edward remained in York while the Nevilles set about reducing these strongholds. The first two were delivered by appointment, and magnificent Bamborough alone held out, till '*Newcastle*, the King's great gun, and *London* the second gun, and *Dijon* a gun of brass, and *Edward* and *Richard* the bombardels, sent the stones of the castle flying unto the sea'.

After that there was nothing left to stay for, and the King started on his journey back to London.

As he rode along, Edward might well muse with satisfaction on his position, both at home and abroad. Recently at York he had concluded a truce with Scotland for fifteen years; Louis XI was bidding for England's friendship with France, though here there was the awkward little matter of the proposed bride; the Pope had sent his congratulations and blessing two years before, and Burgundy had been cordial from the beginning. At home it seemed as though all trouble with the Lancastrians must be at an end. Surely he might now look forward to nothing but enjoyment. If there was a fly in the ointment, it was Warwick. Warwick was altogether too masterful, and his family was too numerous and too powerful. But the Woodvilles were also numerous: if Edward were to make them powerful by judicious marriages, they would be bound to him by their gratitude; and with a bodyguard of Woodvilles might he not defy the Nevilles?

Edward passed through Stony Stratford again before he reached London, and he spent the greater part of the summer within easy distance of Grafton, chiefly at his manor of Penley in the Chilterns. But still nothing was said in public about the marriage, and still Warwick was allowed to continue his negotiations with Louis for the hand of Bona of Savoy. As months passed and nothing happened, Louis became restive, and pressed for a definite date to be named when Warwick would come over and conclude the treaty of peace which was to be sealed with the royal marriage. Warwick promised to come early in October. By the end of the summer strange rumours were flying about which made Warwick very uneasy; and when the Council met at Reading on 14th September, ostensibly to discuss the question of the currency, the King was bluntly requested by his Lords to say when he would marry.

'Then the King answered that of a truth he wished to marry: but perchance his choice might not be to the liking of all present. Then those of the council asked to know his intent, and would be told to what houses he would go. To which the King answered in right merry guise that he would take to wife Dame Elizabeth Grey, the daughter of Lord Rivers. But they answered him that she was not his match, however good and however fair she might be, and that he must know well that she was no wife for such a high prince as himself: for she was not the daughter of a duke or an earl, but her mother, the Duchess of Bedford, had married a simple knight, so that though she was the child of a duchess and the niece of the Count of St Pol, still she was no wife for him. When King Edward heard those sayings of the lords of his blood and his council, which it seemed good to them to lay before him, he answered that he should have no other wife, such was his good pleasure.'[1]

So now the truth was out, and though Warwick fumed, and the lords grumbled and the ladies tossed their heads, nothing could be done about it, except to hope that the King would soon get over his passion, and divorce his wife; and in the meantime everyone decided to hate Elizabeth as much as possible, and to find fault with everything she did. In this happy frame of mind the whole court assembled on Michaelmas Day in the Chapel of Reading Abbey, where Elizabeth was led in by the Duke of Clarence and the Earl of Warwick, and

[1] Waurin, see Oman's *Warwick*, p. 162.

presented to the people as their Queen; she took her place on a throne beside the King and all present knelt before her.[1]

It is obvious that Warwick had been badly treated, but Edward himself may not have been so far wrong in choosing an English Queen. Margaret of Anjou was hated throughout England and another French marriage could not have been popular. The people were still smarting from the disgrace of the English defeats in France; and had it not been for the too rapid advance to wealth and power of the new Queen's family, and the consequent insult to the popular Warwick, the commons of England might well have accepted an English Queen with feelings of national pride. A letter written at this time, and probably addressed to Lord Rivers, by Sir John Howard, says:

'Also, my Lord, I have been in divers places within Norfolk, Suffolk, and Essex, and have communicated this marriage, to feel how the people of the country were disposed; and, in good faith, they are disposed in the best wise, and glad thereof. Also I have been with many divers estates, to feel their hearts; and, in good faith, I found them all right well disposed.'

'In good faith' one must point out that this Sir

[1] Miss Strickland in her *Lives of the Queens of England* gives a long description of this scene, which she bases erroneously on a picture in an illuminated manuscript in the British Museum, the *Anchiennes Chronicques d'Engleterre* made for Edward IV by Jehan de Waurin. Actually the picture is a fanciful representation of the wedding of Edward II, but has nothing whatever to do with the scene at Reading.

THE FIRST QUEEN ELIZABETH

John Howard, afterwards Duke of Norfolk—Shakespeare's Jockey of Norfolk—was at that moment doing his utmost to insinuate himself into the good graces of the Queen's family, so as to get positions for himself and his wife in the royal household; but on the other hand if there had been very strong evidence of the marriage being unpopular, it would merely have been foolish to protest so much to the contrary.

The King and Queen stayed in Reading for some weeks after the announcement of their marriage, during which time the betrothal of the Queen's eldest sister, Margaret, to Lord Maltravers, son and heir of the Earl of Arundel, took place.

This was the first of a series of marriages which were arranged for the Queen's family during the next ten years, and which have caused her to be accused of pride and ambition. It is a little difficult to see why these marriages have aroused such resentment against her; she was only doing what was done by everyone at the time, and surely if she had taken all her good fortune for herself, and done nothing for her family, she might rather have been accused of selfishness and false pride. But nothing that Elizabeth did was right in the eyes of Edward's family and of Warwick: to them she was the upstart adventuress who had ruined all their schemes. Even the observance of court etiquette, which her rank necessitated, was held against her as a proof of her overweening pride, although it is obvious that if she had attempted to alter the age-old ceremonial which regulated the life of kings and queens, her enemies would not have hesitated to say that the circumstances of her birth made it impossible for her to behave in the dignified manner which would have come naturally to a princess.

It is true that Lord Rivers had only recently been raised to the peerage, and it is also true that the Woodville family was not very wealthy; but the brothers and sisters of the Queen, even without considering their royal mother, might be supposed to have acquired a status of their own, while, as for dowries—it is certain that the lords who so eagerly matched their children with the Wood-villes did so in the hope of advancement rather than of financial gain. The Queen's three brothers, Anthony, Richard, and John, all born before 1446, were the next in age to herself; then came Margaret, perhaps about eighteen at the time of her betrothal. She was not married till 1466, so possibly she was younger. Anne became the wife of William Bourchier, eldest son of the Earl of Essex; Jacquetta married John, Lord Strange of Knockin; Joan married Anthony Grey de Ruthin, son and heir of the Earl of Kent. Catherine must have been the family favourite, for she, then probably about ten years old, became the bride of the little Duke of Buckingham, Edward's first cousin and ward. She and her husband were carried on the shoulders of squires in the coronation procession of the Queen. Mary was so young that two years elapsed before her wedding to the son of Lord Herbert. Martha obscurely married a mere Sir John Bromley.

Contumely has also been heaped on Elizabeth

because, two years later, by paying 4,000 marks purchase money, she persuaded the King's eldest sister, the Duchess of Exeter, to break off a match between her daughter Anne Holland and George Neville, Warwick's nephew, and accept Elizabeth's son by her first marriage, Sir Thomas Grey, as a bridegroom for the young heiress of the House of Exeter. But on the other hand the Duchess of Exeter most probably was not tardy in the negotiation. Miss Strickland describes her as 'an atrocious character': she 'divorced and despoiled her first husband, and caused the death of her second'.

Elizabeth seriously offended Warwick by this marriage. Anne Holland was the only child of the Duke of Exeter, who was the next heir of Lancaster after Edward, son of Henry VI. It is easy to see why Warwick and Elizabeth were both anxious to secure this bride: if Edward died without children, Warwick, in his now growing antagonism to Edward, might have been glad to have a Lancastrian trump card up his sleeve. Elizabeth too would prefer to have the card in her own hand rather than in that of her enemies.

All these marriages, if not agreeable to modern minds, were the natural outcome of what was considered wisdom at the time at which they took place. But there is one marriage in the Woodville family which it is hard even for their most anxious protagonist to stomach: that is the marriage of the Queen's third brother, John, to the Duchess of Norfolk, a match stigmatised at the time by William of Worcester as 'maritagiam diabolicum'. John was about twenty, and Katharine, Duchess of Norfolk, was nearly eighty and very wealthy; she was the elder sister of the King's mother, so perhaps John was flattered to become the King's uncle. Some writers have pictured the old lady as being tearfully persuaded into the marriage, but as she had already married three times she may not have minded having just one more husband before she died. Like the Duchess of Bedford, she pleased herself about the choice of her second husband, for after the death of the Duke of Norfolk, she married a plain Thomas Strangeways, Esquire. Surely such a match must have been frowned on by her friends, who probably condemned her as 'doting for love' or 'by wanton affection blinded'. Yet an extremely rich woman of eighty, whose life was nearing its close, would not have to be cautious as to whether she pleased the King or not. She had no need to build up a career by connecting herself with the Queen, and it may be deduced that she was not wholly averse to a handsome young husband; but John Woodville must forfeit all sympathy.

Edward ought now to have journeyed north again to York, where Parliament was assembled; but he was enjoying himself too much at home, so he sent the Earl of Warwick to prorogue Parliament in his place. The King and Queen were to spend Christmas at Eltham, and on their way there, they stayed for a week at Windsor. This, of course, was Elizabeth's first visit, as Queen, to this great fortress and historic house of royalty; but although she may have entered it with feelings of pride, she was probably glad to arrive at the more cheerful and comfortable palace at Eltham.

Eltham was described by Froissart as 'a very magnificent palace which the king (Edward III) possessed, seven miles from London', and it was a favourite residence of the Kings of England for 300 years. Here the Order of the Garter is supposed to have been finally established at a tournament in 1347. An entry, 'For the making of 12 Garters of Blue, embroidered with Gold and Silk, each having the mottoe "Honi soit qui mal y pense" and of making other equipment for the king's joust at Eltham,' is found among the Royal Warrant accounts of that date. The story of the foundation of this order by Edward III, after he had picked up the garter of the Countess of Salisbury, a lady whom he much admired, is among those traditions which are now scouted. A pompous commentator, while denying that such an incident could have been the real reason for creating the Order, has endeavoured to raise the tone by suggesting that 'the King may have picked up a garter at some solemn ball or festivity',—that of his daughter-in-law or of the Queen herself. This depressing version will be rejected by all who love romance. Moreover, in a reign when women 'not the best in the kingdom' appeared at tournaments, 'in divers and wonderful male apparel, . . . and thus proceeded on chosen coursers or other well-groomed horses . . . and so expended and devastated their goods, and vexed their bodies with scurrilous wantonness that . . . they neither feared God nor blushed at the chaste voice of the people,' one must suppose that a tinge of flippancy had entered into the solemn institutions of knighthood.

Froissart came to Eltham in 1395 to present a volume of his writings to the young King Richard II, and he describes the scene in the most vivid manner :

'On Sunday the whole council were gone to London, excepting the King and Sir Richard Sturry and Sir Thomas Percy; these two mentioned me again to the king, who desired to see the book I had brought for him. I presented it to him in his chamber, for I had it with me, and laid it on his bed. He opened it and looked into it with much pleasure. He ought to have been pleased, for it was handsomely written and illuminated, and bound in crimson velvet, with ten silver-gilt studs, and roses of the same in the middle, with two large clasps of silver-gilt, richly worked with roses in the centre. The King asked me what the book treated of; I replied, "Of Love." He was pleased with the answer, and dipped into several places, reading aloud, for he read and spoke French perfectly well, and then gave it to one of his knights, Sir Richard Credon, to carry it to his oratory, and made me acknowledgement for it.' This looks a little as though Richard meant to read *Of Love* when he ought to have been saying his prayers.

Edward and Elizabeth arrived at Eltham on 8th December and on that day the King commanded the treasurer and chamberlains of the

Exchequer to pay £466 13s 4d 'to our right entirely well beloved wife, the Queen, for the expenses of her chamber, wardrobe, and stable against this feast of Christmas next coming'. He himself distributed £207 worth of 'giftings'.[1] If these sums are multiplied by ten some idea may be given of the money that was spent at Eltham during the Christmas festivities, quite apart from the ordinary expenses of the household.

But far greater sums were to be lavished on the Queen's coronation, for which preparations were soon begun. In January, 1465, Edward sent ambassadors to the Court of Philip of Burgundy to tell him that the Queen would be crowned on the Sunday next before Whitsun at Westminster, and to invite him to send representatives to the ceremony. It was a matter of great importance to Edward that the more impressive of the Queen's relations should be present, as well as the good-looking but not royal ones. Consequently it was particularly requested that the Prince Jacques de Luxembourg, the Duchess of Bedford's brother, should attend. The situation in Burgundy was a little uncertain just at that moment, for the friendly Philip was so ill that it was feared he would die, and his son, the Count of Charolais, better known to history as Charles the Bold, favoured Henry VI rather than Edward. However, Jacques de Luxembourg came, not only to the Coronation, but also, in the month of March, on a political mission directed against Louis XI.

[1] Scofield, i, p. 364.

In April another embassy was sent to Burgundy announcing the Coronation tournament, at which the Queen's brother, Anthony, was to be the champion. Anthony had married Elizabeth, the daughter of the King's godfather, Thomas, Lord Scales, who had been a close friend of the Woodvilles for many years, and was one of the four knights who nominated Lord Rivers to the Garter. He was a staunch Lancastrian, and he lost his life in Henry's cause, for at the time of Warwick's victory at Northampton in 1460, Scales defended the Tower of London; but he was so hated by the citizens because he 'cast wild fire into the City, and shot in small guns, and burnt and hurt men and women and children in the streets', that, although Warwick on his triumphant return would have spared Scales's life, he himself thought it more prudent to take sanctuary. 'The Lord Scales, for as much as men of London loved him not, he thought that he might have stand in the more surety in the sanctuary of Westminster than in the Tower. Late in the even he entered a boat with three persons rowing toward Westminster, and a woman to which that knew him ascried him, and anon the boatmen gathered them together and followed him, and fell upon him, and killed him, and cast him on the land beside St Mary Overy. And great pity it was, that so noble and worshipful a knight, and so well approved in the wars of Normandy and France, should die so mischievously.' [1]

Anthony was known as Lord Scales since the

[1] Davies' *English Chronicle*, p. 98.

death of his father-in-law. He seems to have enjoyed some reputation in the lists; he had already received a challenge to break a lance from the Bastard of Burgundy, the champion of that country.

The King and Queen spent Easter at Sheen Palace, and after returning from High Mass in the Chapel the picturesque scene took place which is described in a poetical letter written by Anthony himself.

'Truth it is, that the Wednesday next before the solemn and devout resurrection of our blessed Saviour and Redeemer, for certain causes I drew me near toward the Queen of England and of France, my sovereign lady, to whom I am right humble servant, subject and brother. And as I spoke to her highness on my knees, my bonnet off my head, according to my duty, I know not how it happened, but all the ladies of her court environed me about, and anon I took heed that they had tied above my left knee a band of gold, garnished with precious stones which formed a letter,[1] which, when I had perceived, truth to say, it came nigher to my heart than to my knee; and to this collar was hanging a noble flower of Souvenance, enamelled, and in manner of emprise. And then one of the ladies said to me, full demurely, "That I ought to take a step fitting for the time"; and then each of them withdrew to their places. And I, abashed of this adventure, rose up to thank them for their rich and honourable present; but when I took up my cap, I found in it a letter written

[1] It was a collar of SS, meaning 'Souvenance', or remembrance.

on a fine parchment, sealed and enclosed with a small thread of gold only. Now I thought this letter contained the will of the ladies expressed in writing, and that I should know the adventure which the flower of Souvenance was given me to undertake. Then humbly did I thank the Queen, who of her grace had permitted such honour to be done me in her noble presence, and especially did I thank the ladies for their noble present. I went forthwith to the King of England, my sovereign lord, to show him the emprise, and that he would give me leave of licence to accomplish the contents of the said letter, to bring the adventure of the flower of Souvenance to a conclusion.' [1]

This letter was then taken to the King, who broke the golden thread and commanded the contents to be read aloud, after which he gave his assent to the holding of the Tournament in the following October. Chester Herald carried the challenge to the Court of Burgundy, where he was received and entertained 'daily with a great cheer, as pertained an herald to have'. Chester's message was that if the Bastard could not come to England in October, Lord Scales would wait a year for him. In the presence of his father, the Duke, and his half-brother, the Count of Charolais, Anthony Bastard then touched the flower of souvenance as a token that he accepted the challenge and replied that he would not fail to be in London at the appointed time, unless prevented by war or 'other so lawful letting'. The herald was given as a

[1] *Excerpta Historica.*

reward forty florins and the 'rich furred gown with sables' and 'the doublet of black velvet garnished with arming points, and the slits of the doublet sleeves clasped with clasps of gold' which the Bastard was wearing at the ceremony. These courtesy obliged him to wear, regardless of his size and shape, when he took his leave of the Court of Burgundy, and also when he appeared before the King of England to give an account of his journey.

Chester Herald arrived at Eltham on the very day on which Edward left to go to London for the Coronation of Elizabeth.

CHAPTER V

THE CORONATION OF ELIZABETH

'She had all the royal makings of a queen;
As holy oil, Edward Confessor's crown,
The rod, and bird of peace, and all such emblems
Laid nobly on her: which perform'd, the choir,
With all the choicest music of the kingdom,
Together sung *Te Deum*.'

King Henry VIII

CHAPTER V

THE CORONATION OF ELIZABETH

ON 14th April Edward sent a letter to the 'Mayor of our Citie of London' from 'our Manor of Sheen', in which he stated that 'we have certainly appointed and concluded the Coronation of our most dear and most entirely beloved wife the Queen to be at our palace at Westminster upon the Sunday before Whitsunday next coming: we will and pray you that at the said day and place ye for that cause give your personal attendance there in such apparel as is according to your estate and honour. And that ye leave not this in any wise.'

The King ordered one Gerard van Rye to import for him 'divers jewels of gold and precious stones, against the Coronation of our dear wife the Queen'. The silk trade was then almost entirely in the hands of women, and so Elyn Langwith, a London silk-woman, received £27 10s for material for the Queen's 'chairs, saddle, and pillion'. Matthew Philip, Mayor of London in 1464, supplied a gold cup and basin for which £108 5s 6d was paid. Two cloths of gold, provided by John de Bardi of Florence, cost £280, and 'the plate that the Queen was served with the day of her coronation' cost £20. There is an echo of the ancient art of horse-dealing in the note that 'two bay coursers and a white courser' were bought for the Queen's chair 'at our own price', namely fifty marks.[1]

[1] Scofield, i, p. 375.

On Friday, 24th May, Elizabeth left Eltham Palace and came to London by road. She was met at the foot of Shooters Hill by the mayor and aldermen in scarlet, who conducted her through Southwark to the Tower, where it was the custom for a king or queen to spend a night before being crowned.

In order to reach the Tower the procession had to pass over London Bridge, and here the Bridge Wardens had prepared one of those entertainments which it was their duty to offer if the sovereign was entering London from the south. London Bridge was one of the sights of Europe in those days, with its double row of houses on either side of the roadway, and its numerous narrow arches through which the water swirled dangerously as the tide ebbed. To pass at that time was called 'shooting the Bridge' and was considered so dangerous that most people preferred to land above the Bridge and enter their boats again at Billingsgate.[1]

Before the Queen arrived, the roadway was sprinkled with forty-five loads of sand, at a cost of 4d a load, and the draw-bridge was fumigated at a charge of 3s 4d.

On the south side Elizabeth was first greeted by 'Saint Paul', impersonated by a clerk of St George's, who received 20d for his pains. In a room in one of the houses on the bridge a number of clerks sang.

---

[1] Pepys, in his *Diary*, on 8th August, 1662, gives an amusing description of a Frenchman's first passage through the Bridge: 'When he (the Frenchman) saw the great fall he begun to cross himself and say his prayers in the greatest fear in the world: and, soon as he was over, he swore, "Morbleu! c'est le plus grand plaisir du monde" being the most like a French humour in the world.'

But the chief entertainment was an elaborate pageant which had taken weeks to complete. Eight men worked for twelve days on constructing a stage, during which time they used 5,000 nails. Two men took fifteen days to fix on the ninety-six ells of 'Sultwych' (a coarse cloth) which covered this platform. Materials bought included brushes and hogs' bristles, flour for making paste, vermilion, indigo, red and white lead, verdigris, brazil, and 'pynke yellow' for making paint. The stainers received 12*d* a day for their labours. Other workmen were employed sticking on coloured papers—black and white, gold, green, and 'cinopre' (red). On the stage were eight effigies, six women and two angels, dressed in red and purple buckram. Tailors, who received 12*d* a day, worked for two days cutting out the costumes for these figures, which were fixed on with a thousand pins. Their wigs were made of flax, dyed with an ounce of saffron and for their hands gloves were bought and stuffed with flock. The figures of the women wore fine kerchiefs on their heads; but, best of all, the angels' wings were made with nine hundred peacocks' feathers. Other properties for the angels had to be hired, as well as a representation of the Holy Spirit. Ballads were painted on six boards, which were fastened to the sides of the platform. The work was cheered on with a kilderkin of ale which cost 20*d*, and there was a bill at the Crown next door for 46*s* 10*d*. Besides the inanimate figures in the pageant, two female saints were impersonated by men: the first, in compliment to the Queen, was St Elizabeth, and with her stood Mary Cleophas, whose vigil it was, according to one calendar.

When the Queen arrived before this fantasy, the procession stopped and St Elizabeth greeted her with a speech of welcome. Then she passed on till she came to the chapel of St Thomas à Becket, which had been erected to the memory of the saint by Peter Colechurch, when he built the bridge in the late twelfth century. Becket was a favourite saint of Londoners in the Middle Ages, who looked upon him as a guardian of the place of his birth, and within sixty-five years of his death the Common Seal of the City bore a representation of him with the legend: 'Cease not Thomas to guard me who brought thee forth.'

Pilgrims and other travellers, who crossed the bridge on their way out of London, entered this chapel and prayed for a safe return. Now as the Queen passed, a cantor and his boys were singing for her, and farther on, at the church of St Magnus, others sang too. The Wardens had paid the laundering of their albs and amices.

Thus welcomed by saints, angels, and song, the Queen entered London, where the King was awaiting her.

Edward had come up to the Tower two days before Elizabeth, and in honour of the occasion he created, on Ascension Day, many more Knights of the Bath than he had done at his own coronation. The number varies in different accounts from thirty-seven, when the names are given, to forty-eight when they are not, and probably the larger number is a chronicler's exaggeration. Significant among the names are those of several young noblemen who either already had married, or soon were to marry, the Queen's sisters: the Duke of Buckingham, the Earl of Oxford, Viscount Lyle, Anthony Grey de Ruthin, and Lord Maltravers. The Queen's brothers Richard and John Woodville, and Ralph Josslyn, the mayor of London, were also knighted. The City presented the Queen with 1,000 marks. Next day, Saturday, 25th May, the great procession from the Tower to Westminster took place. Elizabeth rode in a horse litter, carried by two bay horses, and all the new Knights of the Bath rode before her in blue gowns with white silk hoods.

The Queen spent the night at Westminster Palace.

The ceremony next day began in Westminster Hall, where the magnificent procession was formed. First came the King's brother, the Duke of Clarence; riding into the Hall, his horse 'richly trapped head and body to the ground' with trappings 'richly embroidered and garnished with spangles of gold'. Clarence was the Steward. After him came the Earl of Arundel, Constable and Butler, and the Duke of Norfolk, Marshal, both on horses trapped to the ground in cloth of gold. These three cleared a passage through the crowd for the Queen, who now entered under a canopy of cloth of gold, with bells at the corners, borne by the Barons of the Cinque Ports, walking between the Bishop of Durham on her right and the Bishop of Salisbury on her left. She was wearing a mantle of purple and

73

a coronet on her head; her golden hair was floating on her shoulders. Behind her came the Abbot of Westminster. Her train was carried by the dowager Duchess of Buckingham, the sister of the King's mother, who was followed by the Duchess of Suffolk and the Lady Margaret, two of the King's sisters, the Queen's mother, the Duchess of Bedford, and all the other ladies. Holding in her right hand the sceptre of St Edward, and in her left the sceptre of the Realm, and walking barefoot upon ray cloth (striped material), the Queen was conducted from the Hall, and through the cloister which then communicated with the great entrance for State processions in the North Transept. The Duke of Clarence and his fellow officers of State, now dismounted, walked before her, with the little Duke of Buckingham borne on the shoulder of a squire, and all the earls and barons and new-made knights with them. The thirteen duchesses, including the Queen's little sister, the child duchess of Buckingham, also borne on the shoulder of a squire, wore scarlet velvet and ermine: fourteen baronesses followed in scarlet and minever; then twelve lady bannerets, in scarlet.

The great bells rang in the Abbey Belfry, and the little silver-gilt bells tinkled on the canopy as the procession passed along.

From the North door, the Queen was led through the Choir to the High Altar, where she knelt, while the 'solemnity appertaining' was read over her by the Archbishop of Canterbury, and then she 'lay before the altar' while further prayers were said.

74

Oure moost goode and graciouse. Quene Elisabeth;
Soder un to this oure ffraternite: Of oure blissed
ladi. And moder of merci: sanct mary vuyin the
qunter of Em·

ELIZABETH WOODVILLE IN HER CORONATION ROBES

FROM THE ILLUMINATED BOOK OF THE FRATERNITY OF OUR LADY'S ASSUMPTION

[By courtesy of the Worshipful Company of Skinners

After this the 'attire' was reverently taken off her head by 'virgins', and she was annointed by the Archbishop of Canterbury, Thomas Bourchier, the Archbishop of York, George Neville, Warwick's brother, holding the holy unction, and then she was solemnly crowned. She was next 'conveyed unto the place of estate' and enthroned 'with great reverence and solemnity, the Abbot of Westminster waiting upon the Sceptres Spiritual, and the Earl of Essex, upon the Sceptres temporal'. During the reading of the Gospel the Queen held the sceptres, which were afterwards taken again by the Abbot and Earl and carried before the Queen when she went to the High Altar to make her offering. During the Mass the Duchess of Suffolk and the Duchess of Bedford 'reverently at certain time of responses held the crown on her head'. After the Queen had sung 'solemnly Te Deum', the ceremony in the Abbey was over, and the procession re-formed in the same order as before, and passed back through the Hall into the Palace.

The Queen then retired 'unto her chamber and then was new revested in a surcoat of purple and from the chamber was brought betwixt the said two Bishops into the Hall unto her place of estate'. From the manuscript which describes the scene, it would appear that at the Coronation Banquet which followed, only the Archbishop of Canterbury and the King's two sisters actually sat at table with the Queen, the Archbishop 'at all times his service covered (served) as the Queen's'. Before eating the Queen washed; the Duke of Clarence holding the basin (presumably the golden one for which £108 had been paid), the Duke of Suffolk and the Earl of Essex holding the sceptres meanwhile. The Queen, wearing her crown, then seated herself on her throne. Throughout the entire banquet the 'said lords' knelt, holding the sceptres. Two ladies also knelt and handed her a napkin, or 'vayle' as it is called, and when she wished to use it, she herself took off her crown, and put it on again afterwards.

In the body of the Hall were four long tables, apparently running at right angles to the Queen's table. At the table next the wall on the left sat the mayor of London, the aldermen, and 'divers officers and citizens of the same'. At the next table sat the Duchess of Bedford, the Countess of Essex, a paternal aunt of the King's, the Duchess of Norfolk (the elderly bride), the Dowager Duchess of Buckingham and her grandson's little wife, and the other peeresses, and beneath them sat the Knights of the Bath 'new-made'. At the next table sat thirteen Bishops and Abbots, among whom the Bishop of Exeter is mentioned as 'not served': this was because his appointment did not receive the Royal assent till the following month. Beneath them sat the judges, described as 'the Chief Judges of the King's Bench and of the common pleas, the Chief Baron and their fellow judges, and the Barons, Sergeants, and divers others'.

The serving of each course was a matter of the most complicated ceremony, and the meal must have lasted for hours. Before the first course, which consisted of seventeen dishes, a procession was formed which ushered in the food. First came the 'Earls, Barons, and other noble Knights', then the Constable, the Marshal, and the Steward followed, riding their coursers once again. The second course consisted of nineteen dishes, and the third of fifteen dishes, and both were preceded by the same procession as the first, 'and by serving the said course of any dish, the Knights of the Bath new made.'

After the three main courses were finished, wafers were handed round by the Knights of the Bath, and hippocras 'was served in by my Lord Scales, cupbearer. And the Queen's Almoner and a chaplain folded up the tablecloth unto the middle of the table, and before her reverently took it up, and bare it from the table. And at the washing after dinner Sir John Howard laid the surnape before the Queen, the Duke of Norfolk, Marshal of England, went before and commanded. And Sir Gilbert Debenham draweth the surnape after.' The Queen then washed with the same ceremony as at the beginning of the banquet.

'And the Knights of the Bath new made brought the spice plates unto the Cupboard, Sir John Say brought the spice plate unto Sir William Bourchier, son and heir unto the Earl of Essex, and he thereof served the Queen.

'The Duke of Clarence delivered the assay of the spice plate, the Mayor of London bore the cup of wine of void and the cup of assay. And at the coming of every course, and during the service thereof, the trumpets blowing up solemnly.

'And betwixt certain courses the King's minstrels

and the minstrels of other Lords, playing and piping in their instruments, great and small, before the Queen full melodiously and in most solemn wise.

'And the feast done and the table voided, the Queen was brought in to her chamber betwixt the said Bishops of Durham and Salisbury. And the sceptres were borne before her in semblance wise as they were brought in.

'And at the Departing of the Queen from the Hall the Cup of Wine of Void (which) was served unto the Queen, was borne through the Hall before the Mayor of London.'

It was the privilege of the mayor to take away with him this gold cup and stand and to keep it as his perquisite.

The coronation of the next Queen of England not of royal blood, Anne Boleyn, nearly seventy years later, has been described so clearly that it throws a little more light on that of her predecessor.

For instance, it was apparently usual for the Queen to wear her hair loose on her shoulders. In the procession through London her palfry was led behind her chair by her master of the horse, and it may be supposed that the white courser which was bought at the same time as the two bay coursers was to take this part. The canopy of cloth of gold which it was the privilege of the barons of the Cinque Ports to carry at all coronations appears to have been ornamented with four silver-gilt bells, and as these bells are mentioned at the coronation of Edward, presumably Elizabeth's canopy was decorated in this way. The 'veil' referred to above is explained as 'a fine cloth (held) before the Queen's face, whenever she listed to spit, or do otherwise at her pleasure'. When the dinner was over the people were 'commanded to stand still in their places or on their forms, till the Queen had washed. Then she arose and stood in the midst of the Hall, to whom the Earl of Sussex brought a goodly spice-plate, and served her with comfits. After him the lord mayor brought a standing cup of gold, set in a cup of assay: and after she had drunk she gave him the cup, according to the claims of the city, thanking him and his brethren for his pains. Then she went under her canopy, borne over her to the door of her chamber, where she turned about, and gave the canopy, with the golden bells and all, to the barons of the Cinque-Ports, according to their claims, with great thanks for their services. Then the lord mayor passed through Westminster Hall to the barge, and so did all the other noblemen and gentlemen return to their barges, for it was then six o'clock.'

This hour gives an indication of the time that Elizabeth's coronation occupied, for Anne started her day at eight in the morning, and at the banquet 'all the tables in the hall were so quickly served, it was a marvel'. Elizabeth would not be later in starting, but she may not have been so 'quickly served' as Anne, and probably the twilight of early summer was falling when the great company dispersed and rowed in their barges back to London, since, happily for Westminster, it was still in the country then.

A largesse of £20 was proclaimed for Garter King

of Arms and his fellow Kings and Heralds, while a similar amount was distributed among the hundred musicians who were present.

On Monday the celebrations were concluded with a great tournament at Westminster, when the Knights from Luxembourg and Burgundy were able to display their prowess, although they did not carry off the prize, a ruby ring, which was awarded to Lord Stanley. The Belfry at Westminster, which stood where the Guildhall now stands, was let to sightseers.

After her coronation, the Queen was given a house in Smithfield called Ormond's Inn, where she established her household. The post of Chamberlain was given to Lord Berners, brother to the Archbishop of Canterbury, a man who had been on the Yorkist side from the first. He was taken prisoner after the second battle of St Albans and carried off by Margaret to York, where he was fortunate enough to be found still alive several weeks later by Edward when he entered that city after the battle of Towton. Perhaps in gratitude to Margaret for having spared his life, he interceded for the citizens of York, and was instrumental in saving all but a few. Lord Berners received forty pounds a year and forty marks reward. The Master of the Horse was John Woodville, who also received forty pounds. Two Carvers, Sir Humphrey Bourchier and James Haute, were paid forty marks each. The two principal Ladies-in-waiting were the Queen's sister, Anne, now Lady Bourchier, and their sister-in-law,

Elizabeth, Lady Scales: each received forty pounds. Lady Alice Fogge, Lady Elizabeth Ovedale, and Lady Joanna Norreis each received twenty pounds, while seven damsels and two other women attendants received salaries ranging from ten pounds down to five marks. Her confessor was Edward Story, Chancellor of the University of Cambridge, and later Bishop of Carlisle: but he only got ten pounds a year for his pains, while the royal physician received four times as much for his services, which doubtless were more frequently required. Large sums were paid by Edward to his apothecary, and although these may have partly related to his interest in the sister science of alchemy, like most superstitious men he probably dreaded death, and consequently took great care of his health; so the Queen's Physician was as highly paid as anyone in her household. Other officers were her Chancellor, clerk of the signet, receiver-general, attorney-general, and solicitor, and three minstrels.

She had her own council chamber in the New Tower, next the Exchequer. Her little sister's husband, the Duke of Buckingham, and his brother, who were wards of the King's, were placed under her care, and for their maintenance she received five hundred marks a year. A tutor who was hired to teach these little sprigs of the nobility their grammar, a master scholar named John Giles, only got six pounds for services which lasted nearly two years.[1]

[1] Scofield, i, p. 378.

CHAPTER VI

THE HAPPY YEARS

'My love, forbear to fawn upon their frowns:
What danger or what sorrow can befall thee.
So long as Edward is thy constant friend,
And their true sovereign, whom they must obey?
Nay, whom they shall obey, and love thee too
Unless they seek for hatred at my hands:
Which if they do, yet will I keep thee safe,
And they shall feel the vengeance of my wrath.'

King Henry VI, Part 3, Act IV, Scene 1

CHAPTER VI
THE HAPPY YEARS

ONE great figure was notably absent from the coronation, and that was Warwick.

Although Edward endeavoured to compensate the Earl for the favours which he was heaping on the Woodvilles, by raising his brother, George Neville, the Chancellor, to the Archbishopric of York, and although he showed his confidence in Warwick by sending him to prorogue the Parliament at York, Warwick could not help but feel that his influence was no longer paramount; however, it is probable that, at this time, neither he nor the King realised to what an extent the breach between them would widen, nor to what disasters it would lead.

Warwick was undoubtedly the finer character: he had none of that self-indulgent love of pleasure which Edward displayed. He was a stern, strong-minded soldier, just the man to lead a weak and helpless king such as Henry was, but a man who had made a mistake in thinking, when he placed a boy like Edward on the throne, that he had another puppet in his hands. Edward knew what happened to weak kings and he made up his mind from the first to govern the country himself. So that although Warwick was the most powerful noble in the realm, and an extremely forceful personality, he was now to discover that Edward was quite as forceful as himself, and twice as crafty. For a time there was no open breach between them, and Warwick was allowed to continue his negotiations with Louis, although Edward secretly had no intention of giving up the Burgundian alliance, which he far preferred. Consequently Warwick had a good excuse to absent himself from England at the time of the Queen's coronation, and he certainly had no wish to be present at the scene of the Woodvilles' triumph.

France was not then the powerful and united country which it later became, largely owing to the cleverness of Louis XI, for it was still divided into rival states, by its antiquated feudal system. Louis' most important vassal was the Duke of Burgundy, whose lands included the rich Flanders as well as his great duchy; and if Burgundy were to combine with the Duke of Brittany, and other lesser feudal princes, and, above all, if any of them were to form an alliance with England, Louis' position would be very dangerous. This was exactly what did happen, and at the very moment that Warwick arrived in France, these lords banded themselves together into what they termed the League of the Public Weal (although in reality they were only seeking to increase their own power) and openly declared war on Louis. So he was obliged to swallow any resentment which he felt over Edward's marriage, and agree to a truce with England. He promised not to give any further assistance to Margaret, if Edward would agree not to help Burgundy and Brittany.

When Warwick returned from this mission, he was greeted with the news that Henry VI was at last

captured: the poor king had been wandering about
for months in the north of England with three
faithful followers, taking refuge where he could.
Edward and his Queen were at Canterbury when
the news reached them, for two months after the
coronation of Elizabeth, they left London in the
height of summer, on a pilgrimage 'the holy, blissful
martyr for to seek'.   Edward loved Canterbury.
In the year of his accession he made the city a
county, independent of the county of Kent, and he
visited it many times during his reign.   On this
occasion Edward arrived on 13th July, 'at the
second hour before vespers,' and was received
by the Archbishop, Thomas Bourchier, the Prior,
and the monks, in green copes 'cum responsorio:
Summe Trinitati ad hostiam ecclesiie'.   Next
day Elizabeth came 'at the fourth hour before
vespers', and was received by the clergy in white
copes, 'cum responsorio: Audi filia.'   While the
King and Queen and the clergy were thus parading
in pomp and pageantry, Henry was captured in
the county of Lancashire, 'by means of a black
monk of Abingdon,' or in other words by means of
the treachery of his friends.   When the news reached
Canterbury, Edward and Elizabeth went again to
the cathedral, and sang Te Deum and there was a
procession to Becket's tomb.   On 24th July Henry
of Windsor was brought to London.   He rode on
horseback, and his feet were bound to the stirrups
with thongs of leather; Warwick met him at
Islington and led him 'through Cheapside and so
through all the City to the Tower', where he was

kept a prisoner for the next five years. No one can help pitying this poor half-mad king; but it was better for him to live peacefully in the Tower where, though he was under restraint, he was not unkindly treated, than to wander about the country destitute. If only Margaret's pride had not driven her on to regain the kingdom for her son's sake, Henry might have ended his days in peace and comparative comfort; and eventually Edward, who was often generous, might have let him retire to some monastery where his pious soul would have been happy. But only the first act of the tragedy had been played: worse was yet to come.

One more event of interest concerning Elizabeth occurred in 1465. She was asked to become the patroness of a college. Nearly twenty years earlier Margaret of Anjou had founded the College of St Margaret and St Bernard at Cambridge, 'to laud and honour of sex feminine'; the seal of the college shows the figures of these two saints, and owes its elaborate coat of arms to Margaret, with the six quarterings, Hungary, Naples, Jerusalem, De Barre, and Lorraine, so that 'no College in England hath such exchange of coats of arms as this hath'.[1]

But if Margaret was the first patroness, the prime mover of the foundation was a friar named Andrew Dokett who, rightly considering that a seat of learning should not be affected by political factions, hastened to seek the support of the new Queen, when the fortunes of war replaced the House of Lancaster by the House of York. 'I mean Andrew

[1] Fuller: *University of Cambridge*, vol. 36.

Dokett, for forty years first Master of this House, formerly a Friar, Rector of St Botolph's in Cambridge, Principal of St Bernard's Hostel, who gathered much money from well-disposed people, to finish this College, and accounted by some, though not by his purse by his prayers, the Founder thereof. A good and discreet man, who with no sordid but prudential compliance so poised himself in those dangerous times betwixt the successive Kings of Lancaster and York, that he procured the favour of both, so prevailed with Queen Elizabeth, wife of King Edward the fourth, that she perfected what her professed enemy had begun. A good-natured lady, whose estate (whilst a widow) being sequestered for the delinquency of her husband (things, though not words then in fashion) made her more merciful to the miseries of others.'[1]

There is no evidence that Elizabeth had any feelings of animosity towards Margaret of Anjou, who was such a good friend to the Woodvilles; and in later years when Margaret had reached the lowest depths of her misfortunes, and was a prisoner in the Tower, Elizabeth is said to have done what she could for the unhappy queen; so that perhaps the 'good-natured lady' was as much impelled by sympathy as by natural pride to continue the benefaction of her predecessor.

The rival claims of the two queens is now settled by placing the apostrophe after the 's', so that since Elizabeth's day the college is known as Queens': but it was she who gave it the first statutes, on

[1] Ibid.

10th March, 1465, and in these she is referred to as 'the true foundress'. The foundation was enlarged from a President and four fellows, to a President and twelve fellows, who were all to be in priest's orders. A little later, in 1468, she visited the College, and was entertained by the cautious Dokett, and she must have admired what is now the oldest part of the beautiful red brick buildings, the first court and the President's Lodge by the river, which was then the very newest thing in architecture.

A happy result of her patronage is the fine portrait which now hangs in the Combination room[1] at Queens'.

This is no mere fanciful representation of the Queen, but a genuine portrait; and these are rare in the fifteenth century. The unfortunate fashion which prevailed among ladies at the time of straining back their hair, and even plucking it out over the temples, so as to enhance the height of the forehead, was most unbecoming, and in Elizabeth's case it is the more to be regretted as the combined effect of her wonderful red-gold hair and her bright brown eyes is thereby lost: but her delicate features, her exquisite pink and white complexion, and her slender figure, can still be appreciated. When to this was added 'her sobre demeanour lovely looking

---

[1] This picture must not be confused with the eighteenth century copy by Hudson in the Hall, or with an earlier copy in the Gallery at Queens'. An engraving of Hudson's copy forms the frontispiece to Vol. 2, Strickland's *Lives of the Queens of England*, and the second copy is reproduced in *Historical Portraits* (C. R. L. Fletcher and Emery Walker, Oxford, 1909). Neither of these copies can compare with the original picture, certainly one of the finest English portraits of the fifteenth century.

and feminine smiling (neither too wanton nor too humble) besides her tongue so eloquent and her wit so pregnant' it is not surprising that she captivated the heart of the King.

This year was probably the happiest in Elizabeth's life after she became Queen of England. She was expecting a child and naturally hoped for an heir to the throne; Edward was deeply in love with her and willing to do everything that he could to please her; and the jealousy which his partiality for her family aroused had not yet begun to bear its poisonous fruit. The attitude of historians towards the Queen has undoubtedly been influenced by the contemporary opinion of the Woodvilles, which was coloured by envy. It must be remembered that Warwick was a national hero: that the people saw him slighted and set aside in favour of the Queen's relations, and that the nobility were infuriated to find themselves supplanted in the King's favour by a family which had no claims on his gratitude, and had been his enemies.

But in judging Elizabeth, it is also necessary to remember that all this was more Edward's fault than hers; he was headstrong and violent in his emotions, determined to have his own way, and not easily influenced. He was brought up to despise the weakness of a king who had been ruled by others, and he did not mean to be put into leading strings by Warwick. While Edward was a boy, his character was partly formed by the Earl, a man who was then defying his king. Edward knew just what

Warwick's aims were: he had known for years that Warwick meant to get control of the kingdom, and now that Edward was on Henry's throne he was forewarned. His conduct towards his cousin seems ungrateful: it was certainly tactless; but was there room in England for a man of Warwick's domineering disposition, and for a king who was determined to rule himself? The secret of Edward's success lay quite as much in his own personality as in the strength of Warwick's arm; and if his self-confidence was inflated by the adulation which his beauty called forth, his keen brain and subtle disposition gave him cause to rely on himself. But the charm which dazzled his people did not blind Warwick, who had known him so intimately from his boyhood, and who saw in him only the callow fledgling which he himself had helped to mature. To him it seemed that Edward was a strutting young cockerel, doting on his cross-bred pullet of a queen, and surrounded by the very riff-raff of the barnyard. Himself he pictured as a noble eagle. His day was over, but he refused to acknowledge it, and in the end he went down fighting. Edward belonged to the new day which was dawning: he was preparing the way for the Tudor despotism and the Tudor glory: Warwick belonged to the Middle Ages and there was no room for him any longer.

Edward's hope that as Elizabeth had two children by her first marriage she might have 'some other' by him, was not immediately realized; nearly two years passed before their first child was born.

'This year (1466), that is to say the ninth day of the month of February,[1] was Elizabeth, princess, and first child of King Edward, born at Westminster whose christening was done in the Abbey with most solemnity: and the more because the King was assured by his physicians that the Queen was conceived of a prince: and especially one named Master Dominic, by whose council great provision was ordained for christening of the said Prince. Wherefore it was after told, that this Master Dominic, to the intent to have great things and reward of the king, he stood in the second chamber where the Queen travailed, that he might be the first that should bring tidings to the king of the birth of the Prince; and lastly when he heard the child cry he knocked or called secretly at the chamber door and frayned (asked) what the Queen had. To whom he was answered by one of the ladies: "Whatsoever the Queen's grace hath here within, sure it is that a fool standeth there without". And so, confused with this answer, he departed without seeing the King for that time.'[2]

There can be no doubt that at the birth of the child the ancient procedure was followed, which was afterwards carefully written down in all its details by Margaret of Richmond. By that time the prophecy of the 'physicians'—more accurately described as astrologers and soothsayers—that the child would wear the crown, had been fulfilled and the Princess was married to King Henry VII.

[1] 11th February is the date given on her tomb.
[2] Fabyan's Chronicle, p. 655.

93

'Her Highness pleasure being understood as to what chamber she be delivered in, the same must be hung with rich cloth of arras,—sides, roof, windows and all, except one window, where it must be hanged so that she may have light when it pleaseth her.' The Queen then 'took to her chamber', after which no man might approach or come into her presence; 'for women were made all manner of officers, as butlers, sewers, and pages, who received all needful things at the great door of the chamber.'

The magnificent christening, which had been prepared for a son, now took place for the little princess: the only difference being that whereas the Archbishop of Canterbury and nine bishops had been summoned to the baptism of the child 'which the Queen shall bring forth', it was the Archbishop of York who performed the ceremony for the less important baby girl. However, the Earl of Warwick, now again in England, stood godfather, and possibly there may have been some idea of pleasing him in choosing his brother to baptise the princess. The two godmothers were the Duchess of York and the Duchess of Bedford; but the child was not named after either the King's mother or the Queen's mother, nor yet after any Queen of England, but after her own mother, Elizabeth. She was called the Lady Princess, and was looked on by her father as the heir to the throne.

The christening ceremony was followed, not long afterwards, by the Queen's churching, which was attended by some strangers from a far-off

country, one of whom, Gabriel Tetzel, of Nurem-
burg, left an account of the scene. These travellers
were making a tour of the courts of Europe, on a
semi-political mission from the king of Bohemia;
they were disguised as pilgrims.

The chief among them was Leo, Lord of Rozmital,
a brother of the queen of Bohemia, and with him
were a company of lords and knights. When
Edward heard that they were at the court of
Burgundy, he invited them to come over to England,
but as the travellers had never before been nearer
to the sea than 'the coast of Bohemia', they suffered
severely from sickness. However, they were greatly
cheered by the sight of the gorgeous jewels in the
tomb of St Thomas à Becket at Canterbury; indeed,
they were enraptured by everything that they saw
in England, from the innumerable shrines to the
pretty women with long trains to their dresses, and
the agreeable habit of kissing strangers, which was
later to be remarked on by Erasmus.

Edward prepared magnificent lodgings for them
and soon sent a herald to summon them to his Court.
Here they were immensely impressed by the King's
amiability, by his good looks, and by the great
reverence which was paid to him, 'so that even
great lords must kneel before him.' They were
entertained at a banquet, when Edward hung
chains of gold and silver on their necks, and knighted
some of them. Later they were invited to attend
the churching of the Queen. 'In the morning the
Queen went from childbed[1] to the church[2] with a

[1] In Westminster Palace.　　　[2] The Abbey.

splendid procession of many priests, carrying holy relics, and scholars singing and carrying lighted candles. Then followed a great number of ladies; then trumpeters, and other musicians; then two and forty of the Kings singers whose singing was beautiful; then two and forty heralds and pursuivants; then sixty lords and knights. Then came the Queen, led by two dukes, and over her was carried a canopy; her mother followed her with sixty ladies. Then they heard mass sung, and then went back, in the same procession, to the palace. Then all who were in the procession sat down to eat: men, women, and priests, sat down according to their rank, and they filled four halls.'

The King was not present at the banquet and his place was taken by 'the King's greatest Earl' (presumably Warwick) who sat in the King's seat. Rozmital sat at the same table, but two steps below him. A largesse was proclaimed among the heralds and musicians, who walked about among the people crying out the amount which they had received. After the meal was over, the Bohemian lords were taken into the hall where the Queen was dining, and they marvelled at the excessive ceremony. 'So the Queen sits on a costly golden chair, alone at table. The Queen's mother and the King's sister must sit far below. And when the Queen speaks with her mother or the King's sister, then they kneel before her till the Queen drinks water. And not till she has been served with the first course, do the Queen's mother and the King's sister sit down. And her ladies and maidens, and all who served the

Queen at table—and these were all great lords—
must all kneel so long as she eats. And she eat for
three hours, and many costly dishes . . . which it
would take too long to describe, and all were silent,
not a word was spoken. My lord, with his attendants,
stood all the while in a corner and looked on. After
the feast was ended, then a dance began. The Queen
still sat on her throne. Her mother knelt before her;
at times she stood up. The King's sister danced the
most delightful dances, with two dukes, and they
made to the Queen delightful reverences, and no-
where else have I seen such overwhelmingly lovely
ladies. Among them were eight duchesses and
about thirty countesses and the others were all the
daughters of great personages. After the dance
came the King's singers and sang. Besides this my
Lord was allowed to hear the King's singers at his
mass in the King's chapel, and I believe that there
are no better singers in the world than these.' [1]

Besides the visitors from Bohemia, several
embassies were entertained during the first two
years after Elizabeth became queen; for now that it
became apparent that Edward was securely seated
on his throne, and that England was recovering
from her disastrous warfare, many foreign monarchs
began to seek his friendship. Among other ambassadors came one of peculiar interest, the patriarch of
Antioch, sent by the Emperor Frederick. Although
the object of his visit has not transpired, the unusual
presents which he brought with him caused surprise

---

[1] Des Böhmischen Herrn Leo's von Rozmital Ritter-Hof-und Pilger-
Reise durch die Abendlande, pp. 155–7.

H

and delight. These were four dromedaries and two camels, the first ever seen in England before, and probably the last for some time after. These innocent animals were sent to live at the Tower, along with Henry VI and other political prisoners, where the king also kept lions, lionesses, and leopards, for whose 'sustentation' a payment of six-pence a day was made.

Celestial visitors came in the shape of three comets, one in the year 1468, one in 1469, one in 1471. Henry VI was more honoured in his reign, by a visit from the emperor of comets—the as yet unnamed and unidentified Halley's comet—which was described in a chronicle at the time. 'And this same year, in the month of June, was seen stella comata, between the north and the east, extending her beams towards the south. The which star was seen also in the court of Rome, as they reported that came from thence.' But Edward's visitors were important too, because naked-eye comets, so bright as to attract the attention of the man in the street, are rare enough. The contemporary descriptions, however, will hardly be sufficiently accurate to please astronomers, for the first was 'a blazing star in the west, at four feet high by estimation, in the evening going from west towards the south, and so endured for five or six weeks', and the second 'appeared a blazing star in the west, and the blaze thereof like a spearhead'. The third was best of all: 'In the eleventh year of the King, in the beginning of January, there appeared the most marvellous blazing star that had been seen. It arose in the south-east, at two of the clock at midnight, and so continued twelve nights; and it arose easter and easter, till it rose full east, at rather and rather[1]; and so when it rose at plain east, it rose at ten o'clock in the night, and kept his course flaming over England: and it had a white flame of fire fervently burning and it flamed endlong from the east to the west, and not upright, and a great hole therein, whereof the flame came out of. And after six or seven days, it arose north-east, and so backwarder and backwarder; and so endured a fourteen nights, full little changing, going from the north-east to the west, and some time it would seem quenched out, and suddenly it burnt fervently again. And then it was at one time plain north and then it compassed round about the loadstar ... And so the star continued four weeks, till the twentieth day of February: and when it appeared just in the firmament, then it lasted all night, some what descending with a greater smoke on the air. And some men said that the blazings of the said star were of a mile in length. And at twelve days before the vanishing thereof it appeared in the evening, and was down anon within two hours, and ever a colour pale and steadfast; and it kept his course rising west in the north, and so every night it appeared less and less till it was as little as a hazel stick; and so at the last it vanished away the twentieth day of February.'[2]

Shortly after the birth of Princess Elizabeth her grandfather touched the summit of his career when he was appointed Treasurer, and raised to the

[1] Sooner and sooner.   [2] Warkworth's Chronicle.

dignity of an earl. This post had changed hands four times since Edward's accession; and in face of so much criticism of the Woodvilles, it ought to be noted that under Lord Rivers the Rolls were better kept than under any of his predecessors.[1] Edward was a man with a keen eye to finance; in the latter part of his reign he reorganized his household most carefully so as to avoid any waste, and by means of trading himself in wool, and other commodities, he was able to add greatly to his wealth, and to die without leaving vast debts behind him.

The great tournament which was pending between Anthony Woodville and the Bastard of Burgundy did not take place till 1467, for the war between Burgundy and France prevented the Bastard from coming to England any sooner. When at length he was free to fulfil his engagement it was determined that the event should be made memorable in the annals of chivalry. Lists were prepared in Smithfield, 'great and pompous' eighty yards in length and ten in breadth and 'sufficiently sanded as appertaineth'. The field was surrounded by railings and there were 'fair and costly galleries for the ladies and other' and a splendid pavilion for the King, and his nobles. On each side of it were boxes for knights and squires and archers, and opposite was another pavilion for the mayor and city dignitaries.

The King, who was about to open Parliament, rode up to London in state from Sheen. Two miles

---

[1] Ramsey: *York and Lancaster*, vol. ii, p. 321.

outside the city he was met by a great procession of nobles, heralds, and pursuivants, 'with the sound of clarions, trumps, shawms and other', and at St Paul's he was received 'with procession solemn of bishops, many mitred, with incense', who led him into the church where he offered at the high altar. 'And then took his horse and rode through Fleet Street where the Bastard and his fellowship beheld his coming. . . . The Lord Scales bare the sword before the King. And the Lord Scales perceiving (the Bastard) turned his horse suddenly and beheld him: the which was the first sight and knowledge personally between them. And so from thence to Westminster, where the King held and began his Parliament on the morrow after.'

More than a week passed before all preliminaries were settled, but at last, on Friday, 11th June, the great day came.

The King took his place in his pavilion; he was dressed in purple, and wore the Garter, and in his right hand he carried a baton. 'Truly he seemed a person well worthy to be King, for he was a very fine Prince, and tall, and well mannered.' When the King was seated, the Mayor and Aldermen and persons of the Law entered the lists, and as they passed before the King, they knelt down, and the sword, which was carried before the mayor, was lowered in salute. Then came Lord Scales, riding on a splendidly caparisoned horse, and followed by eight other horses, each differently caparisoned, and ridden by pages in 'mantles of green velvet embroidered with goldsmiths work, richly made'.

Scales's own horse was covered from head to feet in a trapper of white cloth of gold, with a cross of St George in crimson velvet, and bordered with a fringe of gold half a foot long. The second was in tawny velvet 'accomplished with many great bells', the others were in purple damask, blue velvet, crimson cloth of gold furred with fine sables, green damask, tawny damask, and the last 'in a long trapper furred with fine ermines and bordered with crimson velvet'. Two helmets were carried before Lord Scales, one by the Duke of Clarence and the other by the Earl of Arundel. Four noble lords carried the weapons—two spears and two swords. The King asked 'the cause of the coming', and Lord Scales replied, 'to accomplish and perform the acts comprised in the articles sent by him to the Bastard of Burgundy.' He was ordered to enter the lists, which he did and then retired to his pavilion, a tent of 'double blue satin, richly embroidered with his letters' and with his arms on a banner above it.

Next came the Bastard with seven 'followers' also marvellously caparisoned: one trapped from head to feet in ermines with reins of sables, and one in sables with reins of ermines; one with a device of goldsmith's work of 'eyes full of larmes' (tears); the others all different. He too stated the reason of his coming and then retired to his tent; a proclamation was read at the four corners of the field, and finally the contest began.

After all these preparations, the actual battle was somewhat disappointing, and the accounts of it vary so much that it is a little difficult to decide exactly what happened. It appears that at the first encounter the champions ran together on horseback with lances, but missed each other. The second encounter was still on horseback, but fought with swords and with vizors up. The Bastard's horse, 'being somewhat dim of sight,' ran its forehead on to a steel spike which Anthony's horse 'by chance or by custom thrust into his nostrils that, for very pain, he fell on one side with his master. The Lord Scales rode about with his sword shaking in his hand till the King ordered the Marshal to help up the Bastard'. It is only fair to Scales to say that one account states that 'he made take off his trapper, showing that his horse had no chamfron', so that possibly it was only the shock of the encounter which upset the Bastard. However, there was no further fighting that day.

Next day the combat was resumed on foot. The weapons proposed were casting spears, but Edward thought them too 'mischievous', and ordained that the two men should fight with axes and daggers. When the King gave the laissez aller 'the Lord Scales opened his pavilion . . . and gave countenance that he was ready with hand and foot and axe and eftsoons changed his axe from hand to hand'. Lord Scales seems to have had the better of the encounter, and at length 'smote the Bastard in the side of his vizor', when the King 'cast down his staff and with a high voice cried Whoo! Notwithstanding, in the departing, there was given two or three great strokes. And so they departed and were brought afore the King's good grace. The Lord Scales fought with his vizor open, which was thought jeopardous: the Lord Bastard fought closed . . . And so they were brought up before the King. He commanded each to take other by the hands and to love together as brothers in arms . . . and they went together into the midst of the field, and so departed each man to his lodging.'[1]

There is no mention of the Queen at the Tournament, and as she was expecting another child in about two months, perhaps she was not present. However, Olivier de la Marche says: 'As for the King and Queen, they had caused a supper to be prepared in the Mercers' Hall, and thither came the ladies: and I assure you that I saw sixty or four score ladies of such noble houses that the least was the daughter of a baron. And the supper was great and plentiful; and Monsieur the Bastard and his people feasted greatly and honourably.' Lesser contests followed on the three subsequent days, and then 'Monsieur the Bastard prayed the ladies to dine on Sunday, and especially the Queen and her sisters; and he made a great rout and a great preparation'. But unfortunately, before Sunday came, news was received that the Bastard's father, Philip of Burgundy, was dead; 'so their pleasures were changed into griefs and tears.'

[1] *Excerpta Historica.*

CHAPTER VII

WARWICK'S REBELLION

'Yet whoso will mark the sequel of this story will manifestly perceive, what murder, what misery, and what troubles, ensued by reason of this marriage: for it cannot be denied that, but for this marriage, King Edward was expulsed the realm, and durst not abide; and for this marriage was the Earl of Warwick and his brother, miserably slain.'

Hall's Chronicle

CHAPTER VII
WARWICK'S REBELLION

THIS happy period of rejoicing and festivity was succeeded by one of dark misgivings and tragedy, in which the hostility of the Nevilles and the Woodvilles came to a climax, with consequences disastrous to both sides, and particularly to Warwick.

In spite of the King's lack of interest, Warwick still continued to further negotiations with France, so that he was absent not only from the Queen's coronation, but also from the tournament at Smithfield. Louis was entertaining him at Rouen in magnificent style, and frantically offering marriages, pensions, and even provinces, in his efforts to win Edward from Burgundy. For although the Bastard came ostensibly to joust, he also came to seek the hand of the King's sister, the Lady Margaret, for the Count of Charolais, who by the death of his father now became Duke of Burgundy; but when Warwick returned to England with ambassadors from France, he found that matters had moved against him strongly in his absence. Suspicions were in the King's mind that Warwick was plotting with Louis on behalf of Margaret of Anjou, and the King had taken the Great Seal from the Chancellor, George Neville. Probably Edward was angered by Louis' apparent belief that Warwick could do just what he liked in England, and he received the ambassadors at Westminster with marked indifference, and then went off to Windsor, where the Queen was

expecting the birth of another child. If disappointment was in store for Louis, so was it also for Edward
and Elizabeth, for their second child was another
daughter. On 12th August, the Princess Mary was
christened at Windsor, and two days later Warwick
accompanied the Frenchmen to the coast, and sent
them back to their master, with the present of a few
dogs, and the vague promise of further negotiations.
Warwick retired to his estates in dudgeon; a treaty
was signed with Burgundy, and the marriage of the
Lady Margaret was announced. On 9th October
Elizabeth was granted an annuity of £400 for the
expenses of her two daughters.

At this point in the story 'false, fleeting, perjured,
Clarence' took the first step along the road which
led to his downfall. He openly allied himself with
Warwick, who now conceived the idea that as
Edward had no son, Clarence might be looked upon
as a likely heir to the throne. Consequently the Earl
offered the hand of his eldest daughter, Isabella, to
the young Duke, who was only too happy to accept
it, for Warwick had no son, and his two daughters
were great heiresses. Edward, who saw which way
the wind blew, forbade the marriage absolutely,
and as a papal dispensation was required owing to
the cousinship of the parties, nothing could be done
in a hurry. But when next Warwick was summoned
to court, he sent back the reply that 'never would he
come again to Council while all his mortal enemies,
who were about the King's person, namely Lord Rivers the Treasurer, and Lord Scales and Lord Herbert
and Sir John Woodville, remained there present.'

When he fought against Henry VI, Warwick did not at first plan to go further than remove, if necessary by force, the men who surrounded the King and who swayed the Council; so now he only determined to get rid of the Wood-villes. But once again he was swept along in a sudden precipitation of events. The news that Warwick and the King had quarrelled caused a flickering of the dying flame of Lancastrian hopes; mysterious risings broke out in different parts of the kingdom, and continued in spite of the severest repression. Warwick worked secretly to prepare the way for his numerous relations to join him when the moment came for a general insurrection.

The King was absolutely misled. Warwick retired to Calais, his old stronghold, and appeared to be quietly settled there with his wife and family. In June, 1469, Edward set out on a progress through East Anglia, meaning to make a pilgrimage to Walsingham, that sacred place, where the pilgrims left their shoes at the Slipper Chapel, a mile outside the town, and walked barefoot to the shrine.

It was thought that Elizabeth would go with him, for a gentleman of her household, James Hawte,[1] wrote to Sir John Paston in May from Windsor,

[1] This gentleman was probably a cousin of the Queen's and a brother of Anne Hawte or Haute, familiar to readers of the Paston Letters as the pretty young lady who lived at Calais, and who could not speak English very well. Sir John, who was something of a lady-killer and was described by a friend as 'the best chooser of a gentlewoman', was betrothed to her, but they never married. In a letter which he wrote to her he said: 'Mistress Annes, I am proud that ye can read English: wherefore I pray you acquaint you with this my lewd (uncouth) hand, for my purpose is that ye shall be more acquainted with it.' The lady's mother seems to have been sister of Earl Rivers and her marriage contract, which is dated 18th July, 1429, is published in *Excerpta Historica*.

where the Court spent Whitsuntide: 'As for the King, as I understand he departeth to Walsingham . . . and the Queen also, if God send her good health.'

Elizabeth was most unhappy, for on 20th March she had given birth to yet another daughter, 'a very handsome daughter, which rejoiced the King and all the nobles exceedingly, though they would have preferred a son.' The baby was christened Cecily after the King's mother. Perhaps the Queen's recovery was slow; at any rate she did not accompany Edward on his pilgrimage, but appears to have gone straight to Fotheringhay to await his arrival. In the meantime Edward was light-heartedly passing through Norfolk; at Norwich he was so pleased with his reception that he promised to come back directly, and bring the Queen with him. So said the Pastons, who were delighted at Edward's visit, for they hoped to interest him in a quarrel which they had with the Duke of Suffolk for pulling down a manor of theirs at Hellesdon, near Norwich. John Paston entertained Lord Scales, and Sir John Woodville and other gentlemen to dinner, and his guests promised to call the King's attention to the ruined property. Alas! when the laughing, jingling cortège passed by Hellesdon, Edward cast his bright eyes upon the place and said 'that he supposed as well that it might fall down by itself, as be plucked down', and that was all the consolation that the Pastons got.

From Walsingham the King went to Fotheringhay, that historic Castle, of which now not one stone remains upon another, so that it is no longer possible to see the rooms in which Edward and Elizabeth lived, or the hall in which Mary Stuart, the granddaughter of their granddaughter, died.

But it was time for Edward's holiday mood to end, and on 7th July, after spending a week with Elizabeth, he moved north, with troops and guns, to quell the disturbances there, and Elizabeth was obliged to pay her visit to Norwich alone. The mayor, John Aubrey, wrote the following letter to the Recorder, Sir Henry Spelman, on the 6th July:

'Right reverent sir, I recommend me to you. Please it you to know, this same day came to me the Sheriff of Norfolk himself, and told me that the Queen shall be at Norwich upon Tuesday seven night surely. And I desired to have know of him, because this should be her first coming hither, how we should be ruled, as well in her receiving, as in her abiding here. And he said, he would not occupy him therewith, but he councilled us to write to you to London . . . and we to be ruled thereafter . . . for he let me to wit that she will desire to be received and attended as worshipfully as ever was Queen afore her . . . And that it please you, if it may be, that at that day ye be here in proper person . . .

'Written in haste at Norwich the VI day of July Anno IX Regis E. quarti

'By your wellwiller

'John Aubry &c.'

But if the Sheriff was too mean, or too discourteous, to trouble himself about the Queen, Norwich was only too delighted to receive her 'worshipfully'. A committee was appointed to organise the entertainment, and they started in the happiest manner by indulging themselves with a ceremonial feast, at the hostelry of one Henry Brad-field, in the city. A man named Parnell, celebrated for his skill in arranging plays and pageants, came over from Ipswich, together with his servants, and stayed for twelve days, during which they devised one of those naïve entertainments with which great personages were greeted at the time. When the great day arrived, messengers darted about the county to find out which road the Queen was taking, and to direct her escort to enter the city by the Westwick Gate, where Patriarchs, Apostles, and Virgins were waiting.

It was a gloomy day and everyone was dreading lest bad weather should spoil the decorations. At length the Queen arrived with her little daughters, of whom the Princess Elizabeth was the only one old enough to take any notice of what was going on. Beside the Gate was a stage, covered with red and green cloth, and adorned with figures of angels, and scutcheons and banners of the King's and Queen's, and besides fourteen square scutcheons, powdered with crowns, roses, and fleur-de-lys. Here were two giants made of wood and leather, their bodies stuffed with hay, and their crests glittering with gold and silver leaf. The Angel Gabriel greeted the Queen, and he was accom-panied by two patriarchs, twelve apostles, and six-teen virgins, in mantles with hoods. A man named Gilbert Sperling had prepared another pageant, perhaps to show what Norwich could do without the assistance of Ipswich, and this represented the Salutation of Mary and Elizabeth, and required a speech of explanation from the producer. Clerks sang, accompanied upon organs, and no doubt the whole thing compared very favourably with the entertainment offered to Elizabeth on London Bridge at her coronation, for Norwich was the second most important city in England at the time, and very wealthy.

But this was only the first part of the Queen's welcome, and, when it was over, she moved on to the house of the Friars Preachers, where she was to stay during her visit. Here at the entrance another splendid pageant was waiting, on a stage with stairs leading up to it, covered with 'tapser work': the great chair of St Luke's Guild had been brought from the Cathedral for the Queen to sit in, and for the use of it the fraternity were careful to charge a considerable sum. Unfortunately there was only time for a choir of boys to sing, before the rain came down in torrents and all the rest of the entertainment had to be abandoned, while the Queen hastily retired into her lodgings, and the citizens flew about in dismay, carrying the costly coverings and ornaments of the stage into a neighbouring house; but even so much damage was done, for which an extra allowance was made on every bill afterwards.[1] The rain was symbolic: dark days lay ahead, and pleasure would be drowned in tears. Warwick's plans were now perfected and, for a blunt soldier, Warwick had been very subtle.

[1] *Norfolk Archæology*, vol. 5, p. 32.

In July, while Edward was at Fotheringhay, Clarence secretly crossed over to Calais, and was married to Isabella Neville by the Archbishop of York, her uncle. The very next day Warwick landed in England, bringing his son-in-law with him. All the scenes of 1460 repeated themselves: the men of Kent flocked to join him; the gates of London were flung open to receive him; and he marched North to confront and to take prisoner his King. Edward was caught between two fires, for although friends were coming to his assistance, before they could reach him they were defeated, and his own small force deserted him in terror. Lord Rivers and Sir John Woodville, whom Edward had sent away from him for their own safety, were found at Chepstow, and were beheaded at Coventry. Edward was surprised in the night, as he lay at Olney, and taken prisoner by the Archbishop of York. He was lodged in Warwick Castle, and then moved to Middleham, in Yorkshire: he was a prisoner, but he was treated with every show of respect; so he hid his feelings and waited.

Warwick's plan had succeeded admirably, but what was he to do now? It became evident that his action in setting himself up against the King was not popular; it was one thing for the men of Kent to rally round him, and nobody minded what happened to the Woodvilles; but the King must be released. The citizens of London were furious, and began to riot, and what was worse the Duke of Burgundy threatened to come over to assist his brother-in-law. Either Warwick must murder

Edward and put Clarence on the throne, or else he must let him go. But the people would never accept the feeble Clarence while Edward lived, and Warwick shrank from killing Edward in cold blood. Somewhere the plan had miscarried. However, Lord Rivers was dead, and that was something, and when at the end of the summer Edward escaped, it was probably because Warwick felt that there was no other way out of a situation which had become impossible.

In October Sir John Paston wrote to his mother that the King was back in London, where he had arrived with a great train of nobles and a thousand men: 'The King himself hath good language of the Lords of Clarence and of Warwick . . . saying they be his best friends; but his household men have other language, so that what shall hastily fall I cannot say.'

Elizabeth left Norwich early in August, and was in London by the 16th, where she remained, keeping 'scant state', till Edward was released. It was not only her father's and brother's deaths which alarmed and grieved her during these dreadful weeks; an attempt was made to undermine the King's affection for her, by reviving the old story that the Duchess of Bedford had used witchcraft to bring about her daughter's marriage. A man named Thomas Wake pretended to have found one of those wax images used by sorcerers to bring about the death of their victims, and he swore that it belonged to the Duchess.

Ridiculous as the accusation undoubtedly was, it was not to be taken lightly, for royal ladies had suffered the penalties of being convicted of witchcraft before, and the penalties were anything but pleasant. Everybody remembered how Duke Humphrey's wife, Eleanor, was made to do penance through the streets of London, in Henry's reign, for a similar charge, and that her supposed accomplices had been hanged. Fortunately the Duchess had done a valuable service for the City, when she interceded with Margaret of Anjou to spare it after the second battle of St Albans, and she now appealed to the mayor and aldermen to protect her if the accusation were brought before the Council. When the matter was finally investigated, Wake could bring no witnesses to support him, and the Duchess was cleared of all suspicion.

For a while after Edward returned to London there was an appearance of peace and goodwill. Clarence managed to insinuate himself into Edward's good graces again, and a general pardon was proclaimed; Warwick was flattered by the betrothal of his nephew to the Princess Elizabeth. But it was not long before a private brawl between some gentlemen in Lincolnshire developed into a serious rising and Edward was obliged to take up arms again. The rising was easily subdued but it was found that Warwick and Clarence were implicated, and all further attempts at friendship were impossible. Once more Warwick made for Calais, but this time in vain: Edward's orders that he was not to be admitted got there first, and the harbour was closed. Unable to believe the news, Warwick waited before the town, tossed in a violent storm, during which the wretched Duchess of Clarence, who was on board, gave birth to a son which died. This event can hardly have softened the feelings of any of the party towards Edward, even if it was not already too late for any hopes of peace.

At this point that evil spirit, Louis XI, chuckling to hear that Edward was in trouble, came on the scene with a plan. Warwick landed at Harfleur, and immediately Louis set about trying to reconcile him with his enemy Margaret, promising to help them if they would join together to restore Henry to the throne. At first it seemed hopeless, for there was too much blood between them; but in the end Louis was successful, even to the point of making Margaret agree that her son, the Prince of Wales, should marry Warwick's younger daughter, Anne, if Henry regained his crown. These difficult negotiations took four months to accomplish, but the subsequent campaign only lasted a fortnight. It seems extraordinary that Edward was unprepared, and that a second time he should allow himself to be drawn away to the north of England by an unimportant rising, got up by Warwick with the express purpose of luring him there. Moreover he entrusted the command of the army to Warwick's brother, Montague, who, because of a private grudge which he owed Edward, immediately turned traitor. All his soldiers declared for Henry.

Warwick and Clarence landed in Devonshire, on 25th September, and proclaimed Henry king.

Supported by thousands from Devon and Cornwall, which had always been Lancastrian strongholds, they marched to London without opposition, and took Henry out of the Tower. Completely deserted by his army, Edward rode from Nottingham to Lynn, and took ship and escaped to Holland; with him went his brother Gloucester, his brother-in-law Anthony Woodville, his great friend Lord Hastings, and Lord Say.

Everything had happened so quickly that no one can have been more astonished than Henry, when he was taken out of his prison chamber in the Tower, 'not worshipfully arrayed as a prince, and not so cleanly kept as should seem such a prince,' and installed in the apartments which the Queen had prepared for her approaching confinement.

When Edward went North he left his wife and children in London, and Elizabeth, who remembered the miserable time she had endured when he was taken prisoner, showed her sense and forethought by putting the Tower in a state of defence. She was once again expecting a child, and Warkworth says that 'she well victualled and fortified the Tower'. There she installed herself with her mother and the three little princesses and waited anxiously for Edward's return. Then she heard that he had fled the country and that Warwick was in England and Margaret was expected—Warwick, who had killed her father and her brother, and Margaret who had told her eight-year-old son to sentence two old men to death after a battle. If the long-awaited prince were born in the midst of

his enemies, could she hope to save his life? She
made up her mind to take sanctuary, and with her
mother and her children, she stole secretly out of the
Tower by night and went up the river to Westminster.

The right to take sanctuary was an ancient
privilege accorded by the Church. Whoever crossed
the threshold of a sanctuary was under the protection of God, and no one, not even the King himself,
could take him out: the punishment for doing so was
excommunication. The only crimes which were not
covered by this right were sacrilege and treason.
Every church or churchyard was held to have this
right, but in England there were about thirty
churches with a special reputation as sanctuaries;
in London St Martin's le Grand and Westminster
Abbey were the most famous. These were the
resorts of murderers, thieves, debtors, and every
kind of criminal; for naturally fearful abuses crept
into the ancient privilege. The sanctuaries were
infested by criminals, who sheltered there by day
and crept out at night to perpetrate more offences.
'Rich men run thither with poor men's goods; there
they build; there they spend, and bid their credi-
tors go whistle them. Men's wives run thither with
their husband's plate, and say they dare not abide
with their husbands for beating. Thieves bring
thither their stolen goods, and there lie thereon.'
In 1447 the Goldsmiths' Company were pained and
surprised to find that a quantity of false gold and
silver plate had been issued from the privileged
precincts of St Martin's sanctuary, and sold in

London for genuine. The facts were brought to the notice of the King, who wrote to the Dean the following letter: 'Trusty and well beloved, we greet you well, and let you to wit that we be informed that there be divers persons dwelling within our sanctuary of St Martin's, that forge and sell laton and copper, some gilt and some silvered, for gold and silver unto the great deceipt of our liege people.'. . .

However, all criminals did not have such an easy time of it, and sometimes men were so closely watched by their enemies that their only hope of ever getting out alive was to fly the kingdom. In this case 'let the felon be brought to the church door and there be assigned unto him a port, near or far off, and a time appointed to him to go out of the realm.' Then he was given a cross to carry in his hand, and was protected in this way, till he got out of the kingdom; and he might not return without the King's 'special grace'.

There was a special ceremonial attached to the actual taking of sanctuary, which varied according to the church at which it took place, but it was always necessary for the criminal to register himself in the sanctuary book. At Durham the Galilee bell was tolled, the culprit made a full confession, witnesses were called, and all names entered in full. At Beverley there were no witnesses, but the culprit, after confessing his crime, took an oath to keep the peace, to help in case of fire, and to attend mass and ring the bells on the commemoration day of St Athelstane, the benefactor of the church. At Westminster, where the act was called 'taking

Westminster', not only the Abbey but also the whole Close was Sanctuary and all the houses within the precincts enjoyed the same privilege. In the Middle Ages the Close was bounded by a high wall, and it covered all that space now known as Parliament Square and Broad Sanctuary. Some have thought that there was a special building called the Sanctuary, but this was probably only because they saw the remains of the old Belfry, a square tower like a keep, the base of which was still standing in the eighteenth century. Behind the Abbey church lay the Abbey buildings, and between them and the river was Westminster Palace; in the Abbey wall opposite the Palace was a postern through which the Queen and her children must have entered into sanctuary.

It was a strange thing for a Queen of England to register herself and her children among these criminals, but poor Elizabeth was now only 'the Queen that was'. She took up her abode 'assuring her person only by the great franchise of that holy place, in right great trouble, and sorrow, and heaviness, which she sustained with all manner of patience that belonged to any creature, and as constantly as hath been seen at any time, any of so high estate to endure'.[1]

Even though she was safe herself she did what she could for Edward, and sent to the mayor and aldermen to entreat them to hold the Tower for him; but they were not soldiers, and they had to consider what was best for the City, so after allowing

[1] Fleetwood: *History of the Arrival of Edward IV.*

everyone who was in the Tower to take their goods
and go into sanctuary, they handed it over to the
emissaries of Warwick.

It is not known where the Queen was lodged, but
the kindly Abbot supplied her with the necessaries
of life, sending her 'half a loaf and two muttons'
daily, so that although she is described as being 'in
great penury and forsaken of all her friends', yet
perhaps if so much mutton could be consumed in
one day, it must be supposed that some faithful
attendants were with her. In any case one feels
tempted to paraphrase Prince Hal's exclamation:
'O monstrous! but one halfpenny-worth of bread to
this intolerable deal of—mutton.'

After a few weeks it became apparent that Warwick had no intention of wreaking vengeance on
the Queen herself, much as he hated her family.
A butcher named William Gould was allowed to
supply 'half a beef and two muttons every week'
for the 'sustentation' of her household, and the
Council even appointed Lady Scrope to wait upon
her during her confinement, and paid the lady ten
pounds for this service; her physician Domenico
de Sirago, and a midwife named Margaret Cobbe,[1]
were also with her.

[1] Miss Strickland says: 'Mother Cobbe, a well-disposed midwife,
resident in the sanctuary, charitably assisted the distressed queen in the
hour of her maternal peril, and acted as nurse to the little prince,' and
Dean Stanley says in *Memorials of Westminster Abbey*: 'The nurse in the
Sanctuary assisted at the birth.' Apart from the absurdity of a nurse
being kept in a sanctuary, a note in the *Wardrobe Accounts of Edward IV*
(Nicolas) states that Margaret Cobbe, wife of John Cobbe, midwife to
the Queen, was granted a salary of £10 a year, on 15th April, 1469. This
date was a month after the birth of the Princess Cecily, the Queen's
previous child, and, if correct, disposes of Mother Cobbe's charitable
disposition.

And so, in the first week of November, the long hoped-for heir of York at last saw the light of day. He was born in a prison, and he died in a prison, 'this fair son, called Edward, which was with small pomp, like a poor man's child, christened; the godfathers being the Abbot and the Prior of Westminster, and the godmother the Lady Scrope.'

Edward was a man whose best qualities were brought out by danger and adversity. He had thrown away his kingdom through lack of foresight —through too little attention to business and too much attention to pleasure: now he proceeded to regain it with determined courage and brilliant strategy.

He stayed in Burgundy for six months, living on the bounty of his brother-in-law; but Charles was in a difficult position because, now that Louis was certain of England's friendship, war between France and Burgundy seemed inevitable. However, Edward had a friend in his sister Margaret, who did much to persuade her husband to help, and eventually a large sum of money and some ships were provided. Further hope came from the way-ward Clarence, who now began to repent of his treachery; he was far from pleased at the marriage arranged between Henry's son and Warwick's daughter, which removed him farther from the throne than he was before. He wrote to his brother and promised to join him, if he landed in England.

In March, 1471, Edward left Flushing and was driven by a great storm up the east coast to Yorkshire. He landed at Ravenspur, which might have been considered a happy omen, for it was here that Bolingbroke had landed seventy years before, but Yorkshire was not the best place to be in, because its feeling was strongly Lancastrian. In his desperation, Edward resorted to falsehood and swore before the High Altar in York Minster that 'he never would again take upon himself to be king of England', and cried 'King Harry and Prince Edward!' before the assembled people.

He had with him about two thousand men when he landed in England, and he knew that if only he could get to London all would be well; so, he daringly eluded the armies which moved against him, marched past Warwick, who was at Coventry, joined Clarence and his troops, and entered London without fighting one battle.

Warwick hoped that London would resist for a few days, while he hurried after Edward, but the citizens, and particularly their wives, far preferred the handsome, liberal king, who spent so much money, to the one who 'sat upon his throne, limp and helpless as a sack of wool'. Besides, Edward had borrowed large sums from them, and their only hope of seeing themselves repaid lay in his restoration. Not a blow was struck. Two thousand faithful followers poured out of the sanctuaries to greet him, and even poor Henry— pitifully offering to embrace the man who, for the second time, came to take his throne—said: 'My cousin of York, you are very welcome. I know that in your hands my life will not be in danger.'

Edward, on nearing London, had sent 'comfortable messages to the Queen', and he only stayed to give thanks in St Paul's, and to commit Henry to the Tower, once more, before he got into his barge and rowed up the river to Westminster. He entered the Abbey and 'there honoured, and made his devout prayers, and gave thanks to God, Saint Peter and Saint Edward'; and after the Archbishop of Canterbury had placed the crown once more on his head, he hastened to the Sanctuary, where Elizabeth awaited him, with her little daughters, and 'a fair son, a prince, wherewith she presented him at his coming, to his heart's singular comfort and gladness. From thence that night the King returned to London, and the Queen with him, and lodged at the lodging [1] of my lady, his mother, where they heard divine service that night and upon the morrow, Good Friday'.

Happy as Edward and his family must have been to find themselves reunited, they knew that it was not for long. Warwick was advancing on London, and Margaret would invade England at any moment. On Good Friday Edward held a council, and on Saturday he marched out of London to encounter Warwick. Queen Elizabeth, with her mother, and her children and the two Archbishops, went to the Tower.

Edward had fought the battle of Towton on a Palm Sunday, and now on Easter Sunday he fought

[1] Baynard's Castle.

the battle of Barnet. It was a strange encounter, for
it took place in so dense a fog, that no one knew how
the day was going. On Saturday night Edward
crept up in the dark and 'lodged him, and all his
host' so close to the enemy, that Warwick, 'thinking
to have annoyed the King,' spent the whole night
pounding away with his artillery, but the shots
passed harmlessly over Edward's men, 'who kept
them still, without any manner of language.' But
in the dim and misty morning, it was found that
Warwick's line outflanked Edward's at one end,
while Edward's outflanked Warwick's at the other.
Edward's left wing was routed, and the fugitives
fled to London, with the news that the battle was
lost. Poor Queen! she must have felt that her joy
would be short-lived.

But in the meantime, Gloucester, on the right,
was pressing on, and Edward and Clarence, in the
centre, fought valiantly. Then came the turning-
point of the day, for the Earl of Oxford, who had
been pursuing the fugitives from Edward's left wing,
returned behind his own lines; but as his men wore
the badge of a flaming star, it was mistaken in the
fog for the flaming sun of York, and their own com-
rades fell upon them. In the confusion, the day
was lost to Warwick. He leapt on his horse and fled
into a wood, but he was caught and killed, before
Edward could reach him to save his life. The great
King-maker had fought his last battle. His brother
Montague was also killed, and their bodies were
taken to St Paul's, and exposed to the public, so that
no one might say afterwards that Warwick was still

alive and thus cause further trouble to be 'seditiousely sown, and blown about the land'.

It was thought at the time by superstitious people that the fog at Barnet was brought by magic, but Fabyan, in his chronicle, will not commit himself beyond saying: 'Of the mists and other impediments which fell upon the lord's party by reason of the incantations of Friar Bungay, as the fame went, we list not to write.'

The battle was over by ten o'clock and Edward returned triumphantly to London to give thanks at St Paul's and to comfort Elizabeth.

But still all was not over, for just when it was too late, Margaret and Prince Edward landed. If only she had come while Warwick was still alive, things might have gone otherwise, but now it was well-nigh hopeless. She herself would rather have turned back when she heard the news, caring only to preserve the life of her son, but her friends persuaded her to go on. Many flocked to her standard from Devon and Cornwall as she made her way up through Taunton, Glastonbury, and Wells, to Bristol, and so into Gloucestershire. Here, at Tewkesbury, her army was utterly defeated. Worse still, it seemed as though a spirit of ruthless revenge had taken possession of the King. When Prince Edward was taken prisoner after the battle, he was cruelly put to death. Margaret gave herself up to her conqueror; perhaps she hoped to join her husband in the Tower. She had nothing else left to live for, and her proud spirit was utterly broken.

While Edward was in the West defeating the

last hopes of Lancaster, Elizabeth and her children were suddenly exposed to great danger in London. A bastard of the house of Neville, a man named Falconbridge, a sea-captain of Warwick's, conceived the idea of taking London in Edward's absence, and of putting Henry on the throne again. He came over from Calais with about three hundred followers, and the men of Kent, who seemed ever ready to rise in Warwick's cause—even though he was now dead — joined Falconbridge in large numbers. He endeavoured to make a peaceful entry into the city, but when he found the gates closed against him he determined to attack it. 'As this was doing, over came from London fresh tidings to the king, from the Lords, and the citizens, which with great instance, moved the King, in all possible haste, to approach, and come to the city, in the defence of the Queen, then being in the Tower of London, my lord Prince, and my Ladies, his daughters, and of the Lords, and of the City, which, as they all wrote, was likely to stand in the greatest jeopardy that ever they stood in.'

Edward sent 1,500 men 'well beseen, for the comfort of the Queen, the Lords, and the citizens'. Hasty preparations were made to defend the City, and, in the struggle which followed, the Queen's brother, Anthony, now Earl Rivers, greatly distinguished himself. Falconbridge attacked at Aldgate and at Bishopsgate, and burnt several houses on the Bridge, 'and so, after continuing of much shot of guns and arrows, a great while upon both parties, the Earl Rivers, that was with the Queen in the

Tower of London, gathered unto him a fellowship of four or five hundred men, and issued out at a postern upon them, and, came upon the Kentish men, being about the assaulting of Aldgate, and mightily laid upon them with arrows, and upon them with hands, and so killed and took many of them, driving them from the same gate to the water side.' After this defeat Falconbridge withdrew.

On 21st May Edward entered London in state. The Duke of Gloucester rode before him with many Lords, and the Duke of Clarence behind him. Last of all came Margaret. No daisies were seen in any hats that day, and though she went to the Tower, she did not see her husband. While all at Court were feasting and rejoicing that night, Gloucester stole away to a 'bloody supper in the Tower'. It was given out, next day, that Henry died of 'pure displeasure and melancholy' on hearing of his son's death, and his wife's capture, but it was generally believed that he was murdered by Gloucester's hand, and with Edward's consent.

On the morrow Henry's body lay in state in St Paul's, but only his face was exposed, 'and in his lying he bled upon the pavement there.'

CHAPTER VIII

CLARENCE AND GLOUCESTER—THE SEIGNEUR DE LA GRUTHUYSE

'Gives not the hawthorn bush a sweeter shade
To shepherds looking on their silly sheep,
Than doth a rich-embroider'd canopy
To kings that fear their subjects' treachery?'

King Henry VI

CLARENCE AND GLOUCESTER—THE SEIGNEUR DE LA GRUTHUYSE

ONE of Edward's first actions on resuming the throne was to create his son Prince of Wales. On 3rd July the two archbishops, eight bishops, and a number of lords and gentlemen, took an oath of allegiance to the boy, swearing to accept him as 'the very and undoubted heir' if he should 'happen to overlive' his father.

Edward showed the love and respect which he had for his wife by putting her at the head of the Prince's council; the other members were the Archbishop of Canterbury, the Dukes of Clarence and Gloucester, the Bishops of Durham and Bath and Wells, and Anthony Woodville, who on the death of his father became Earl Rivers. They were 'to be of council unto the said Prince, giving unto them, and every four of them, with the advice and express consent of the Queen, large power to advise and council the said Prince', and to administer his estates until he reached the age of fourteen.

Abbot Mylling was rewarded for his kindness to the Queen by being appointed chancellor to his godson; nor were lesser friends forgotten, for William Gould, the butcher who supplied Elizabeth and her family with meat while they were in sanctuary, was granted special trading rights as a recompense. Edward wrote the following letter to the Keeper of the Privy Seal:

'For the great kindness and true heart that our

well-beloved William Gould, citizen of London, butcher, showed unto us and unto our dearest wife the Queen, in our last absence out of this Realm, every week, then giving unto her for the sustentation of her household half a beef and two muttons: and also after our field of Tewkesbury, at her being in the Tower, brought a hundred oxen into a meadow beside our said Tower for the killing of the same, whereof the Kentishmen, . . . our rebels, shipmen, took of the said beasts fifty . . . to his great hurt and damage, we have given and granted unto the said William . . . our Letters of Licence, that he may charge a Ship called the Trinity of London . . . with ox-hides, lead, tallow, and all other merchandises except stapleware (wool) . . . to go out of this our said Realm into what parts beyond the sea it shall like him . . .' Good William! One hopes he did well and that his ship prospered.

In September Edward went on one of his many pilgrimages to Canterbury, and the Queen went with him. He had good reason to give thanks, and apparently many other people thought so too, for Sir John Paston wrote on 28th September: 'As for tidings the King and Queen, and much other people, are ridden and gone to Canterbury; never so much people seen in Pilgrimage heretofore at once, as men say.' It must have been a cheering sight to see the ancient city crowded with the gaily dressed ladies and gentlemen who followed in the train of the King and Queen, and Canterbury was glad to receive Edward, now that he came in a holiday mood, for only three months before he had

THE FIRST QUEEN ELIZABETH

been there to punish traitors who joined in Falconbridge's rebellion.

The King and Queen spent the following winter
at Westminster, and as it was the first Christmas
since Edward's 'last absence out of the realm', as
he airily called it, they celebrated the festival in
public. The King and Queen went to the Abbey to
hear mass, wearing their crowns, and 'the King
kept his estate in the White Hall. The Bishop of
Rochester which sang high mass . . . sat at the King's
board on the right hand, and the Duke of Buckingham on the left hand. On New Year's day the King
and Queen went in procession, and were not
crowned; the King kept none estate in the hall.
On Twelfth Day the King and Queen went a procession: the King crowned, and the Queen not
crowned, because she was great with child. He
kept his estate in the White Hall, the Bishop of
Rochester on his right hand, the Earls of Shrewsbury and of Essex on the left hand.'

In February the Court moved to Sheen, a palace
which had been given to Elizabeth for life shortly
after her marriage. It was then a fortified manor
surrounded by a moat; but it was burned down in
the reign of Henry VII, and was later rebuilt by
him, and called Richmond. Time has swept away
nearly all the homes in which Elizabeth lived:
Grafton has been rebuilt; Westminster, Fotheringhay, Greenwich, and Sheen are gone; Ludlow is
in ruins; the interiors of Windsor and the Tower
have been altered, and only a fragment of Eltham
remains. Westminster Hall still shows the scene of

public processions and banquets in which she took part; but the rooms in which she passed her private life are all gone.

It was at Sheen that Edward III died, after his mistress, Alice Ferrers, had drawn the rings from his fingers and left him alone; and here, too, Anne of Bohemia died and her young husband Richard II 'took her death so heavily that besides cursing the place where she died he did also for anger throw down the buildings unto which the former kings being wearied of the City were wont for pleasure to resort'. Sad as this was it benefited Elizabeth, because the palace was rebuilt by Henry V and Henry VI and so was comparatively modern when it came into her possession.

On 17th February, 1472, Sir John Paston wrote: 'Yesterday the King and Queen, my Lords of Clarence and Gloucester, went to Sheen to pardon; men say not all in charity; what will fall men cannot say.' Unfortunately the happiness which Edward's restoration occasioned to his family was broken by a violent quarrel between his two brothers. Clarence was jealous of Gloucester, who not unnaturally was more highly regarded for his loyalty to Edward than Clarence for his tardy repentance. Clarence's treachery in trying to steal the crown might be forgiven, but it could hardly be forgotten. Now Gloucester wanted to marry Anne Neville, the girl who had been betrothed to Henry's son, because by doing so he hoped to inherit half the great estates of her father, the Earl of Warwick; but Clarence was determined to stop the match. It was his intention to inherit the earldom and all the estates. Edward sided with his younger brother, partly because there was no reason against the marriage, and partly because he did not want so much wealth to pass into the hands of one man, and that man Clarence. The Queen sided with Gloucester too; she hated and distrusted Clarence because through his folly her father had lost his life, and her husband had nearly lost his throne.

The quarrel became so serious that people thought the brothers would take up arms against each other. It is said that Clarence disguised his sister-in-law as a servant, and hid her in the house of a citizen in London, and that Gloucester found her, and persuaded her to go into sanctuary. Clarence then sulkily agreed that his brother should have Anne, 'but that they should part no livlihood'; and it was just at this stage of the affair that the royal family went down to Sheen, 'for pleasure to resort.' Edward pronounced judgment: he said that Gloucester should marry Anne, and that the estates must be divided. But to console Clarence, the Great Chamberlainship was given to him, and the Lieutenancy of Ireland; Gloucester was made Constable of England and Warden of the Forest North of the Trent. The one person who was not consulted was the widowed Countess of Warwick, to whom most of the lands belonged. She had been in sanctuary at Beaulieu Abbey ever since her husband's death, and from this refuge she wrote letters 'in her own hand . . . in the absence of

clerks' to every member of the royal family, even
to the six-year-old Princess Elizabeth, to ask for
justice; but the chance of getting hold of all this
wealth was not to be resisted, and it was finally
decided that 'the Countess of Warwick was no more
to be considered as to her inheritance than if she
were dead'. It seemed as though no one had any
conscience where money was concerned, and not the
least disagreeable part of this sordid squabble was
the youth of the two dukes: Clarence was twenty-
two and Gloucester nineteen.

Young though he was, Gloucester now became
the most important man in England after Edward,
and he was certainly the cleverest. As time passed
the king relied more and more on his youngest
brother, and had it not been for the accident of
Edward's early death, which gave Richard the
opportunity to indulge his insane ambition, he might
have been remembered as a brave soldier and a
brilliant statesman, without the added stigma of
being the murderer of his brother's children.

The King and Queen were at Windsor in April
and there Elizabeth gave birth to another daughter,
the Princess Margaret, who only lived for eight
months, and was buried in Westminster Abbey in
the following December. A month after the birth
of this child, the Duchess of Bedford died, which
must have been a great grief to Elizabeth and to
all her family. This handsome, energetic woman
had devoted her life to her husband and children,
but the shock of Lord Rivers' execution, and the
anxiety through which she had passed during

Warwick's rebellion, probably hastened her death. She was fifty-six years old.

Elizabeth had other troubles at this time. Although her greatest enemy, the Earl of Warwick, was dead, she felt that she had a secret enemy in Lord Hastings, the King's Chamberlain and lifelong friend. Sir Thomas More draws a rather attractive picture of him as a gallant and honourable man, 'a good knight and a gentle, of great authority with his prince, of living somewhat dissolute, . . . a loving man and passing well beloved.' But it would seem that he was not passing well beloved by the Queen, who was jealous 'of the great favour that the King bare him, and also for that she thought him secretly familiar with the king in wanton company'. Hastings had one great merit: he was absolutely loyal to Edward. But he pandered to the King's amorous disposition; in fact it is quite likely that it was he who first drew the King's attention to Elizabeth's beauty, for shortly before the royal marriage, he was a party with her in one of those matrimonial arrangements so typical of the time, by which Elizabeth's eldest son, Thomas Grey, was betrothed to the as yet unborn daughter of Lord Hastings. Hastings' dislike for the Queen may have originated when this contract was ignored and her son betrothed to Anne Holland, the King's niece.

When Edward returned from his exile in Holland, Elizabeth found that Hastings' influence over him had increased during the months which they had passed in close companionship; and probably her

THE FIRST QUEEN ELIZABETH

dislike for Hastings was intensified when her husband, shortly afterwards, took the Lieutenancy of Calais away from her brother Anthony and gave it to Lord Hastings. It is a little difficult to arrive at an estimate of Anthony's character; he appears to have been a somewhat fastidious and romantically minded man, probably not at all in sympathy with Edward's excursions into wanton company; his thoughts were set on antiquated deeds of chivalry 'and beauty making beautiful old rhyme, in praise of ladies dead and lovely knights'. Edward showed his appreciation of his brother-in-law's moral character when he chose him to bring up the Prince of Wales, but he was impatient with his unpractical preoccupations.

Directly after the battles of Barnet and Tewkesbury, Anthony announced his intention of going on a pilgrimage; not a very sensible suggestion when the country was in such a state of unrest, and when every true man was needed to help in the task of bringing order out of chaos. Edward was furious, and in his hot-headed way rated Anthony soundly. Sir John Paston wrote to his mother: 'The King is not best pleased with him for that he desireth to depart; in so much that the King hath said of him that whenever he hath most to do, then the Lord Scales will soonest ask leave to depart and weeneth that it is most because of cowardice.' In September Paston wrote again that 'the Lord Rivers hath licence of the King to go to Portingale'. But Anthony thought it wiser to defer his pilgrimage, although he was granted a safe conduct on 12th

October, in which he was styled *Carissimus ac Dilectissimus Consanguinius*; but the Lieutenancy of Calais remained with Hastings.

Elizabeth may have had another reason for hating Hastings if it was he who discovered Jane Shore, the London mercer's wife, who was Edward's most celebrated mistress: Hastings was known to have been in love with her, but 'he forbare her, for reverance towards his King, or else of a certain kind of fidelity towards his friend'. During the short interval which elapsed between Edward's death and his own, she lived under his protection. A man who was as fond of his pleasure as Edward was not likely to resist a woman like Jane Shore, a merry, witty creature, true sister to Nell Gwynne; and if Edward was to have a mistress, which seemed inevitable, he was fortunate to find one with such a generous nature. His connection with her appears to have lasted for many years, and the story that it was she who saved Eton College, when Edward contemplated appropriating its revenues, is well known.

Sir Thomas More, who knew her in later life, wrote of her: 'This woman was born in London, worshipfully friended, honestly brought up, and very well married, saving somewhat too soon. Her husband, an honest citizen, young and goodly, and of good substance. Proper she was and fair: nothing in her body that you would have changed but if you would have wished her somewhat higher. Thus say they that knew her in her youth . . . Yet delighted not men so much in her beauty as in her

pleasant behaviour. For a proper wit had she and
could both read well and write, merry in company,
ready and quick of answer, neither mute nor full
of babble, sometime taunting without displeasure
and not without disport. In whom the King therefore took special pleasure. Whose favour to say
truth she never abused to any man's hurt but to
many a man's comfort and relief. Where the King
took displeasure she would mitigate and appease
his mind; where men were out of favour she would
bring them in his grace . . . In many weighty suits
she stood many men in great stead either for none or
very small rewards, and those rather gay than rich
. . . for wanton women and wealthy be not always
covetous.'

Edward, who had a sense of humour of a rollick-
ing description, was wont to say 'that he had three
concubines, which in three diverse properties
diversely excelled. One was the merriest, another
the wiliest, the third the holiest harlot in his realm,
as one whom no man could get out of church
lightly to any place, but it were to his bed.' The
merriest was Jane Shore, but the names of the other
two ladies are unknown, though it may be surmised that the holy one was Elizabeth Lucy, the
mother of my lord Bastard, Arthur Plantagenet. In
passing, it is interesting to notice that Edward's
grandson, Henry VIII, also had a bastard son called
Arthur, though why this sacred name of Arthur
was bestowed on bastards is a mystery.

Although in the old but very late ballad about
Jane Shore she is made to say:

'Long time I lived in the Court
With lords and ladies of great sort,'

it is most unlikely that she did anything of the kind
or that she was ever present at any of the festivities
which the King and Queen held.

Fortunately a description of one of these court
functions survives, and as it is one of the few opportunities which there are to get a glimpse of Elizabeth's life at this time it is of great interest. This
detailed account of the visit of a foreign nobleman to
Windsor, in the autumn of 1472, was written by a
man whose name is unknown but who held the
position of Bluemantle Pursuivant.

When Edward was obliged to flee from England
in 1470 he narrowly escaped being captured by the
Easterlings—the merchants of the Hanseatic League
—who were then at war with France and England.
He was chased by their fleet, but fortunately his own
ships were so small that they were able to sail into
the shallow harbour at Alkmaar in Holland, at
low tide, where the larger ships of the Easterlings
could not follow. The Lord of Gruthuyse, the
Governor of Holland, hearing with surprise that the
little ships just arrived had on board the King of
England and his suite, immediately received Edward
on land, and so saved him from being taken
prisoner when the tide rose. Gruthuyse took Edward
to his house at the Hague and entertained him there
during his exile, and Edward now desired to repay
this hospitality by bestowing an earldom on his
kind host.

The Seigneur de la Gruthuyse arrived in September and was honourably received at Dover. When he came to Canterbury 'he was presented with wine, capons, Pheasants, Partridges, and other Presents, such as they had in those Religious Places, both of Christchurch and Saint Augustin. The mayor and his brethren presented him also with such dainties as they had. Also when he came to Rochester he was presented by the mayor and his brethren with wine, capons, Pheasants, Partridges: and after supper with fruit and sweet wine'.

From Rochester, where he stayed the night, he proceeded next day to Gravesend where he was 're-presented with sweet wine'. The King was not in London, but Gruthuyse was welcomed by the sheriffs and entertained to 'an honourable and plenteous dinner', and afterwards conveyed by boat to Westminster, where he was given lodgings in the house of the Dean of St Stephens, in Cannon Row. From there, within two days, he was summoned to Windsor.

The description of the castle and the entertainment is well worth quoting in full as it gives a rare glimpse into the private life of the King and Queen. The King had prepared 'on the far side of the quadrant[1] three chambers richly hung with cloth of Arras, and with beds of estate, and when he had spoken with the Kings grace, and with the Queen, he was accompanied to his chamber by the lord Chamberlain, and Sir John Parr, with divers more, which supped with him in his chamber: also there

[1] Quadrangle.

supped with him his servants. When they had supped, my lord chamberlain had him again to the King's chamber. Then incontinent the King had him to the queen's chamber, where she had there her ladies playing at the marteaux, and some of her ladies and gentlewomen at the Closheys (ninepins) of ivory, and Dancing. And some at divers other games, according. The which sight was full pleasant to them. Also the King danced with my lady Elizabeth, his eldest daughter. That done, the night passed over, they went to his chamber. The lord Gruthuyse took leave, and my lord chamberlain with divers other nobles, accompanied him to his chamber, where they departed for that night. And in the morning, when Matins was done, the King heard in his own chapel our lady mass, which was melodiously sung, the lord Gruthuyse being present. When the mass was done, the King gave the said Lord Gruthuyse a Cup of Gold, garnished with Pearl. In the midst of the cup is a great piece of a Unicorn's horn,[1] to my estimation seven inches compass. And on the cover was a great Sapphire. Then he went to his chamber, where he had his breakfast. And when he had broken his fast, the King came to the quadrant. My lord Prince also, borne by his Chamberlain, called Master Vaughan, which bade the foresaid Lord Gruthuyse welcome.

'Then the King had him and all his company into the little Park, where he made him to have a great sport. And there the King made him to ride on his

---

[1] A charm against poison. Presumably the cup was made out of a segment of horn, mounted in gold.

L

own horse, a right fiery hobby, the which the King gave him. And there in the Park the King gave him a royal Crossbow, the string of silk, the case covered with velvet of the King's colours, and his arms and badges thereupon. Also the heads of the quarrels were gilt. The King's dinner was ordained in the Lodge, but before dinner they killed no game, saving a doe; the which the King gave to the servants of the foresaid Lord Gruthuyse. And when the King had dined, they went an hunting again. And by the castle they found certain deer lying: some with greyhounds, and some run to death with buckhounds. There were slain half a dozen Bucks, the which the King gave to the said Lord Gruthuyse. By that time it was near night, yet the King showed him his garden, and Vineyard of Pleasure, and so turned into the Castle again, where they heard evensong in their chambers.

'The Queen did to be ordained a great Banquet in her own chamber. At which Banquet were the King, the Queen, my lady Elizabeth, the King's eldest daughter, the Duchess of Exeter, the Lady Rivers, and the Lord Gruthuyse, sitting at one mess, and at the same table sat the Duke of Buckingham my lady his wife with divers other Ladies my Lord Halifax, chamberlain to the King, my lord Berners, chamberlain to the Queen, the son of the foresaid Lord of Gruthuyse, master George Bartte, secretary to the Duke of Burgundy, Lois Stacy, usher to the Duke of Burgundy: also certain other nobles of the King's own court. Item, there was a side table, at which sat a great view of ladies, all on the one side. Also

146

in the outer chamber sat the Queen's gentlewomen, all on one side. And on the other side of the table, over against them, sat the lord of Gruthuyse's servants . . .

'And when they had supped, my lady Elizabeth, the King's eldest daughter, danced with the Duke of Buckingham, and divers other ladies also. Then about nine of the clock, the King and the Queen, with her ladies and gentlewomen, brought the said Lord Gruthuyse to three chambers of Pleasure, all hanged with white silk and linen cloth, and all the floors covered with carpets. There was ordained a bed for himself, of as good down as could be gotten, the sheets of Reynes,[1] also fine fustians[2]; the counter-point cloth of gold, furred with ermine, the Tester and the Ceiler also shining cloth of gold, the curtains white sarsenet; as for his head Suit and Pillows, (they) were of the queen's own ordinance. Item, in the second chamber was an other (bed) of estate, the which was all white. Also in the same chamber was made a Couch with feather beds, hanged with a Tent, knit like a net, and there was a Cupboard. Item, in the third chamber was ordained a Bayne[3] or two, which were covered with Tents of white cloth. And when the King and Queen, with all her ladies and gentlewomen, had showed him these chambers, they turned again to their own chambers, and left the said lord Gruthuyse there, accompanied with my lord chamberlain, which dispoiled (disrobed) him and went both to the Bayne . . . And when they had been in their Baynes as long as was their pleasure,

[1] Fine linen made at Rennes, in Brittany.
[2] Blankets.
[3] Bath.

they had green ginger, divers Syrups, Comfits and Hyppocras; and then they went to bed. And on the Morn he took his Cup of the King and Queen, and turned to Westminster again, accompanied with certain knights, esquires, and other of the King's servants, home to his lodging. And on Saint Edward's day openly in the Parliament chamber was created Earl of Winchester.'

A few days later the King and Queen came back to Westminster, and Parliament was opened on 13th October. 'About ten of the clock before noon, the King came into the Parliament chamber in his Parliament robes, and on his head a Cap of maintenance; and sat in his most royal majesty, having before him his lords Spiritual and Temporal.'

This session is of interest where Elizabeth is concerned, because the Speaker made a special reference to her. He said that it was the intent and desire of the commons to commend 'the womanly behaviour and the great constancy of the Queen' while the King was 'beyond the sea'. He then referred to the 'Joy and Surety' to the land which the Prince's birth had occasioned, and to the 'knightly demeaning' of the Dukes of Clarence and of Gloucester; to the constancy of Lord Rivers and Lord Hastings and others; and particularly to the 'humanity and kindness' of Lord Gruthuyse in giving hospitality to the king during his exile. The King then left the Parliament chamber to change into the habiliments of an earl; in this attire, and still wearing his crown, he returned to the Parliament Chamber to create Gruthuyse Earl of Winchester.

When this ceremony was over the King went into the White Hall, and there the Queen joined him, wearing her crown. Behind her came the little Prince of Wales, wearing his Robes of Estate, and carried in the arms of his chamberlain, Master Vaughan. A procession was formed, and the great company passed into the Abbey, 'and so up to the shrine of Saint Edward, where they offered.' After the service the King held a banquet in the White Hall, and the Bishop of Lincoln, who had sung High Mass, sat on the King's right hand, and the Duke of Clarence and the new Earl of Winchester, on his left. Many bishops and noblemen were present and Gruthuyse gave a largesse to Garter King of Arms, which was, however, cried by Norroy because Garter had an impediment in his speech: a fact which caused Edward great amusement, and indeed it seems a most unfortunate failing in a herald. After Edward had washed and graces were said, he concluded the festivity by creating a King of Arms. The day was now over; it was six o'clock, and the new Earl took his leave and returned to his lodgings.

CHAPTER IX

WAR WITH FRANCE—DEATH OF CLARENCE

'Why strew'st thou sugar on that bottled spider,
Whose deadly web ensnareth thee about?'
King Richard III

WAR WITH FRANCE—DEATH OF CLARENCE

THE Seigneur de la Gruthuyse may have thought, from his reception, that England was in a very prosperous and peaceful condition, but in reality the country was still in a disturbed state, and particularly in the West. Early in the spring of the following year, 1473, the Queen and the Prince of Wales were sent to Hereford to hold an Assize, accompanied by a body of royal commissioners.

On 2nd April Sir John Paston wrote to his brother: 'Men say the Queen with the Prince shall come out of Wales, and keep this Easter with the King at Leicester, and some say neither of them shall come there.' In Norwich a soothsayer named Hogan predicted a rebellion in May, and Paston's comment on this was: 'As for the world I wot not what it meaneth, men say here, as well as Hogan, that we shall have ado in haste.' So it was decided that it would be beneficial to the King's peace for the three-year-old Prince to remain in the Welsh Marshes, and he went to live in Ludlow Castle, 'that by the authority of his presence the wild Welshmen should refrain from their accustomed murders and outrages.''

The King spent the whole summer moving about the country, to inspire confidence and prevent disorder; but he came to Ludlow in June to establish the Prince in his new home, and a little later elaborate ordinances were drawn up to regulate the boy's life. John Alcock, Bishop of Rochester, was appointed his teacher, and Lord Rivers his Governor, but one would imagine that his nurse, Avice Welles, was more necessary to his person at this time and that the rules for his conduct were devised for future use. The Prince was to rise 'at a convenient hour according to his age' and no one was to come into his room till he was dressed, but Lord Rivers, or his chamberlain, or his chaplain; and he must hear mattins in his chamber and then go to mass in the chapel; 'on the principal feasts, sermons to be preached before him.' After breakfast he was 'to be occupied in such virtuous learning as his age shall suffer to receive'. At dinner: 'to be reasonably served by worshipful folks wearing our livery. That no man sit at his board, but as Earl Rivers shall allow, and that there be read before him such noble stories as behoveth a prince to understand: and that the communication at all times in his presence be of virtue, honour, cunning, wisdom, and deeds of worship, and of nothing that shall stir him to vice.' After dinner he must spend two hours at his lessons and then only might he 'be shewed such convenient disports and exercises as belong to his estate to have experience in'; after this he heard evensong, and then his attendants were 'to enforce themselves to make him merry towards his bed'. His curtains were drawn at eight o'clock and 'a sure and good watch to be kept about his person'. Yet it was all for nothing; all this watch, and care and love, and foresight, was wasted. Because of the ambition of a little crooked, malignant devil, this lovely, fair-headed boy, his father's 'most desired treasure', was lost.

In August Elizabeth was at Shrewsbury with the King, and there she gave birth to her second son, who was christened Richard, presumably after his grandfather, the Duke of York, whose title was bestowed on the boy nine months later. The succession was now made doubly sure, and the dynasty of York was safely established. It might seem that Edward had little left to wish for, yet at this moment he chose to go to war with France. His chief motive was the hope that if Englishmen were indulged with their favourite sport, a war with France, they would forget their grievances at home; and in this he proved right, for when he proceeded to invite contributions for this purpose the money poured in. There was no reason for the war: the whole thing was absurd, but Englishmen were burning to avenge themselves on the old enemy, and this sentiment was mixed with the less elevated one of selfish greed.

Edward had entered into some sort of an agreement to help his brother-in-law, the Duke of Burgundy, who spent his whole life struggling against France. The whole of the year 1474 was employed by Edward in travelling about the country, collecting 'benevolences', as these free-will offerings were called. He had the gift of remembering the names and faces of his subjects, which, coupled with his affable manners, stood him in good stead. An Italian who was in England at the time wrote: 'I have frequently seen our neighbours here, who were summoned before the King, and when they went they looked as if they were going to the gallows. When they returned, they were joyful, saying that they had spoken to the King, and he had spoken to them so benignly that they did not regret the money they had paid: . . . when anyone went before him he gave him a welcome as if he had known him always.'[1] He asked a rich old lady what she would give him towards the war, and when she said, 'For thy lovely face, thou shalt have twenty pounds,' he kissed her: whereupon she doubled the amount.

Preparations went on apace; but before Edward could leave England he had to make sure of Scotland's neutrality. So the hand of his third daughter, Cecily, was offered to the infant son of James III. The eldest daughter of the King of England was too good a match for the Prince of Scotland and her father had something better in view for her; the second daughter must be kept in reserve; but the third daughter would do well enough. So, with a marriage portion of twenty thousand marks, the fair Cecily, aged five, the fairest of all Edward's fair daughters, was betrothed to Prince James, aged three, and Scotland was bribed to temporary friendship. Treaties with other countries were hastily renewed, and nothing remained but for Burgundy to give the signal to advance. Unfortunately Charles, better called the Rash than the Bold, was carrying on a little war in the Upper Rhine, and wasting the

[1] *Calendar of Milanese Papers,* vol. i, p. 193.

strength which he should have saved for his attack on France. He kept Edward waiting so long, that the people of England began to wonder if the war would come to anything in the end. But Edward secretly meant to be crowned at Rheims; that was to be his personal satisfaction; and anyway he dared not disappoint his subjects, who had so willingly given him their money. So a council was appointed to rule the country in his absence and the Prince of Wales was brought from Ludlow, for he was to be Keeper of the Realm during his father's absence. The little boy made a state entry into London. On Whit Sunday he was knighted, and then he was given into his mother's care. The Queen was granted two thousand pounds a year for the expenses of her household, and a similar sum for the expenses of the Prince.

At length, on 30th May, Edward departed, and the whole city turned out to bid him farewell and to conduct him to London Bridge, whence he took ship to Greenwich, and then proceeded by way of Canterbury to Sandwich. Before he finally embarked he made his will. It is a very long document, as might be supposed, but it contains some interesting items relating to the Queen and her children. To the Queen Edward left 'all our goods, that is to say, bedding, arrases, tapestries, verdours, stuff of our household, ornaments of our Chapel, with books appertaining to the same, plate and jewels excepted, . . . and over this we will that our said wife, the Queen, have and enjoy all her own goods, chattels, stuff, bedding, arrases, tapestries, verdours, stuff of household plate and jewels, and all other thing which she now hath and occupieth, to dispose it freely at her will and pleasure without let or interruption of our executors'. To his daughters, Elizabeth and Mary, he left marriage portions of ten thousand marks each, if they were 'governed and ruled in their marriages by our dearest wife the Queen, and by our son the Prince, if God fortune him to come to age of discretion'. A similar provision was made for a child which the Queen was expecting 'if God fortune it to be a daughter'. Cecily was to have the eighteen thousand marks still owing on her dowry, towards another marriage, if anything happened to stop her marriage to the Prince of Scotland. Among the names of the executors that of 'our said dearest and most entirely beloved wife, Elizabeth, the Queen' comes first.

So now there was nothing more to see to in England, and Edward embarked for France, with a splendid army, and all the latest implements of war; but as to the war itself it is best described in the paragraph which summarises the year 1475 in *The Chronicle of London*: 'The King . . . passed to Calais, and so forth into Picardy: and there, upon a bridge, King Lewis of France and he spake together, and took appointment betwixt them of certain marriages, and certain money in hand, and fifty thousand crowns of sterling money yearly to be sent to the King out of France . . . and the King returned again over to England.' As there was no real reason for the war, there was no spirit to animate either the army or its leaders. When the Duke of Burgundy arrived, after much delay, it was found that his army was in such a wretched condition that it was useless. Charles had wasted his resources in the Upper Rhine, and so had lost his best chance of emancipating himself from Louis by combining with Edward's magnificent army, the largest and best equipped which had ever landed in France. Edward hesitated, uncertain what to do.

Elizabeth's uncle, the Comte de St Pol, the treasured royal relative who graced her coronation with his presence, had already promised that if the English soldiers would advance to St Quentin, where he was, he would hand the town over to them. The Comte de St Pol was in a difficult position because, although he was the uncle of the Queen of England, he was also Constable of France, a vassal of King Louis, and a next-door neighbour of the Duke of Burgundy's: so he thought the simplest way out of the difficulty was to deceive each one in turn. Edward advanced to St Quentin, only to find that the gates were closed against him and the artillery trained upon him. His army was threatened with starvation, because Louis had taken the precaution of devastating the counties of Artois and Picardy. The weather was terrible; Edward caught a tertian fever which never afterwards left him; Charles was a broken reed; the whole expedition was most disappointing.

In the meantime the King of France was working underground to discover means of pacifying Edward, for he feared Edward far more than he feared Charles; secretly he bribed every Englishman whose palm he could reach, and it soon came to Edward's ears that Louis was willing to pay handsomely for peace. Accordingly it was arranged that the two kings should meet on a bridge over the Somme, at Picquigny; but in order to prevent any treachery a strong wooden lattice was erected in the middle of it. Edward marched to Amiens with his whole army, and on 29th August, in pouring rain, the two Kings exchanged a Judas kiss, through a little wooden grating on the bridge.

De Commines was with Louis and he remarked on Edward's 'noble and majestic person, but a little inclining to corpulence. I had seen him before, when the Earl of Warwick drove him out of his kingdom: then I thought him much handsomer and, to the best of my remembrance, my eyes had never beheld a more handsome person'. This was half the secret for the failure of the enterprise: the fire of Edward's youth was gone. Urgent necessity might have aroused him to his old energetic self. If Louis had invaded England, the Edward of Mortimer's Cross, and Tewkesbury, and Barnet, would have met him; but this bastard war, without a motive, sounded no note that was loud enough to rouse his sleeping spirit; and indeed nothing would ever rouse it again. Although so lately he had camped upon the field of Agincourt, he agreed to take money to end a war in which not one battle was fought.

At least he had the satisfaction of knowing that it was he who laid down the conditions for peace;

Louis must pay him 75,000 crowns immediately, to settle the cost of the expedition, and a yearly sum of 50,000 crowns during the rest of his life. Margaret of Anjou was to be ransomed with a further 50,000 crowns, and finally the Dauphin was to be betrothed to the Princess Elizabeth or, if she died, then to her sister Mary. So that if nothing was lost except honour, something at least was gained; and if Elizabeth would never be Queen of France, her daughter might be one day. The one person who suffered from the expedition was the Comte de St Pol, because soon afterwards Louis sent for him with loving words, and had him beheaded. The war was over.

Two months after Edward's return to England Elizabeth gave birth to her fifth daughter, on 2nd November, 1475. She was christened Anne. This was a new name for a princess of England, but it was a significant one to the House of York, for Edward traced his claim to the throne through his grandmother Anne Mortimer. It was also the name of Edward's eldest sister, Anne, the Duchess of Exeter, who may perhaps have been the new princess's godmother; but if so it was not for long, as this 'atrocious character' died in the following year. The Princess Anne was only three years old when her father betrothed her to the son of the Archduke Maximilian of Austria, with a dowry of 100,000 crowns: a larger amount than had been allotted to his elder children. About two years later (the date is uncertain) another son was born

161   M

at Windsor, and was called George, after his worth-
less uncle the Duke of Clarence; and a few months
later he also received the lieutenancy of Ireland when
the same uncle unwillingly closed his disastrous
career. But the little boy did not enjoy this honour
long, for he died during a severe visitation of the
plague which occurred in 1479.

Poor Clarence had rushed upon his fate. He may
have been a drunkard, which would not have im-
proved his spirits or his temper; and when his wife died
in 1476 his mind appeared affected by his grief. Two
months later Charles the Bold was killed in battle, and
he left his dukedom and his vast wealth to his only
daughter Mary; Clarence felt that he might be con-
soled if he could marry this tremendous heiress. He
had never recovered his temper after Gloucester's
marriage, but he would be appeased if he could
make this brilliant match. His sister Margaret,
Charles's widow, the new Duchess's stepmother,
fostered the plan, for Clarence was her favourite
brother; when she left England, ten years before,
he was still a charming, handsome boy of nineteen,
and she had not suffered from his failings as the
rest of his family did. But Edward was far from
wanting his irresponsible brother to be put into a
position where he could meddle with the affairs of
Europe, and Elizabeth seems to have foolishly
hoped that her brother Anthony, now a widower,
might be accepted as a husband by the young
Duchess; while Louis of France, who wanted Burgundy more than anything else, secretly offered the
hand of the six-year-old Dauphin, in defiance of his

treaty with Edward. Mary of Burgundy was twelve
years of age and quite capable of choosing for herself. She wanted a husband old enough to protect
her, not a child of six; nor did she want a husband
with the reputation of Clarence, nor yet one so far
beneath her in rank as Lord Rivers. She had
already decided to make a very suitable marriage
with the Archduke Maximilian of Austria, son of
the Emperor Frederic III.

Clarence was so enraged by his disappointment,
for which he blamed Elizabeth, that he became
reckless, and determined to be revenged. His wife
had died after giving birth to a child, but he now
declared that she was poisoned or bewitched. The
accusation was certainly aimed at the Queen and
this was the last way to get into Edward's good
graces. He was very angry, for Clarence had
'used a King's power' in the matter, since the trial
was only carried out by the Justices of the Peace
at the Petty Sessions. In his turn Edward laid a
charge of sorcery against three friends of Clarence's,
two of whom were hanged. There seems something
of feminine spite in this; it must have been Elizabeth's reply to the outrageous suggestion that she
had tried to murder her sister-in-law; for Edward
had more serious grounds of complaint against
Clarence, which he soon brought to light. But
Clarence was reckless: nothing could keep him
quiet. After his two friends had been executed he
brought before the Privy Council the priest who had
received the dying confessions of the victims, and
as this man had preached the restoration of

Henry VI, Edward felt the time had come to send his brother to the Tower.

No one would say a good word for Clarence now: he had his friends in different parts of the country, sufficient in number to make Edward nervous, but at the Court there were none. The Queen had well-grounded reasons for hating him, and it must be conceded, although it cannot be proved, that she did all she could to turn her husband against this 'rash, intruding fool'. Gloucester would never raise a finger to save his brother, whose death would remove one more obstacle between him and the Crown, which was as much the loadstar of his life as ever it was of Clarence's; moreover if Clarence were dead Gloucester could hope for some more of those lands and titles which had been the source of their previous quarrel. Hastings, Rivers, and all the rest never ceased to din into Edward's ears the fact that Clarence was disloyal, and though Edward took the blame for Clarence's fate he always regretted it, and would say in after years: 'Oh! unfortunate brother, for whose life not one creature would make intercession!'

Edward himself accused Clarence before Parliament. All his past crimes were recalled and to these were added his more recent misdemeanours, pale indeed beside what was already forgiven, but which were now described as 'much higher, much more malicious, more unnatural and loathely treason'.

He was accused of slandering the King by saying that he practised necromancy, of proclaiming the

King a bastard, of pressing those claims to the succession which were settled on him during Henry VI's short second reign, and of plotting to send his son out of the kingdom to raise up enemies against the King. Clarence's son was only three years old, and if his father thought that his wife and younger son were poisoned, he probably sought to save his only remaining son from a similar fate; but it was a serious thing to allege that the King was a bastard for it involved not only Edward's honour but also his mother's. The improbable story that Edward was not the son of his father, but of a handsome archer, persisted throughout his life, and was used later by his loving brother Gloucester. It is likely that Clarence also spread rumours about Edward's own marriage, saying that Edward was already betrothed at the time he married Elizabeth; and though this was not publicly stated at the trial it would have had more effect on the King than any other of Clarence's crimes, for not only was he absolutely loyal to Elizabeth, but any question involving the validity of their marriage also involved the legitimacy of their children.

No one accused Clarence but Edward, and no one defended him. Clarence was condemned to death by Parliament. Yet Edward recoiled from a public execution and perhaps he hoped that someone would intercede for his brother's life. Then Parliament pressed that the sentence should be carried out, and one more was added to the dark secrets of the Tower; those secrets which leaked out through chinks and crannies, which nothing could keep hidden, and which spread like smoke through London, and through England, and through Europe.

'O Lord! methought what pain it was to drown! What dreadful noise of water in mine ears!'

For whether Clarence was drowned in wine or water, everyone believed that he was drowned; and if he is remembered for nothing else, he is remembered for the butt of malmsey.

If Elizabeth was instrumental in bringing about Clarence's death, it was Gloucester who chiefly profited by it, for he again became Great Chamberlain, and the title of Earl of Salisbury, which Clarence had borne since 1472, was given to Gloucester's only son, while the Lieutenancy of Ireland went to the infant Prince George. A Milanese gentleman at the court of Louis XI wrote some months later: 'I hear nothing from England except that for the time being they live at peace with the king here, and keep the cloth of those that are drowned.'

CHAPTER X
COURT LIFE—DEATH OF EDWARD

I had enough, I held me not content,
  Without remembrance that I should die;
And more ever to encroach ready was I bent,
  I knew not how long I should it occupy;
I made the Tower strong, I wist not why;
  I knew not to whom I purchased Tattersall;
I amended Dover on the mountain high,
  And London I provoked to fortify the wall;
I made Nottingham a place full royal,
  Windsor, and Eltham, and many other mo;
Yet at the last I went from them all,
  Et, ecce, nunc in pulvere dormio!

Skelton

COURT LIFE—DEATH OF EDWARD

THE death of Clarence may have cast a shadow over Edward's life, but it cast no shadow over the Court, which was the most brilliant since the days of Edward III. But although it was luxurious and magnificent, the court of Edward and Elizabeth was also orderly and refined: the domestic arrangements of the household were regulated in every detail, and the duties of each officer and servant, with the amount of food, firing, and lighting, allowed, were set down in the *Liber Niger Domus Edw. IV.* The Queen, of course, had her separate establishment, which was similar to the King's, though on a smaller scale. From the pages of this book it is possible to form a clear idea of the daily life in the royal palaces.

Three meals a day were served, breakfast, dinner, and supper; and the amount of bread and wine, and the number of dishes, was regulated for each person. For breakfast the King had two loaves, made into four manchets, 'one mess of kitchen gross', and half a gallon of ale. At noon, if there was 'no press of lords or strangers', he was served with eight dishes: his lords in hall and chamber with five; his other gentlemen in court with three dishes, besides porridge; and grooms and others, with 'two dishes diverse'. . . . 'Bread and drinkings for the King's person betwixt meals, cannot be ascertained but by record of the ushers of the chamber.' The number of pitchers of wine and gallons of ale served with each meal was fixed, and provision of 'one pitcher, half gallon measure' was allowed for the nightly ceremony of the bedmaking. Candles and torches were apportioned 'when the day shorteneth'; also logs for his fire 'one chimney day and night burning for winter season: and if there be more needful chimneys to burn for the King's honour in the great chamber, then as the chamberlain and usher think reasonable'. Among the numerous officers of the court were the secretary, the four chaplains, the esquires, gentlemen ushers, yeomen, officers of the wardrobe and the beds, grooms of the chamber, minstrels, pages, and many besides. The doctor of physic 'standeth much in the king's presence at his meals, councilling and answering to the King's grace which diet is best, and to tell the nature and operation of all the meats. And much he should talk with the steward, chamberlain, assewer, and the master cook, to devise by council what meats or drinks is best according with the King.' The barber when he plied 'his instrumental tools' was only to do it in the presence of a knight or squire of the chamber. A watchman, called a wait, 'nightly from Michaelmas till Shere Thursday, pipeth the watch within this court four times, and in the summer nights three times: and he to make bon gait at every chamber door and office, as well for fire as for pickers and perils.' The Children of the Chapel were carefully provided for and 'when they be grown to the age of eighteen years, and then their voices be changed and they cannot be preferred within this Chapel nor this Court, the number being full, then if they will assent, the King assigneth every such child to a College of Oxford or Cambridge of the King's foundation there, to be in finding and study sufficiently, till the King otherwise like to advance him'. A Master of Grammar was kept to instruct them, and he was to be a priest, so that he could also assist in the Chapel.

The minstrels were in constant attendance on the King and the Queen and the Prince of Wales; each had their own company, 'whereof some use trumpets, some shawms and small pipes, and some as string men.' There were thirteen of them and they were required to be present at court at the five great festivals of the year, 'to blowings and pipings for the King and his household at meats and suppers.' Two were always in attendance, 'being present to warn at the King's ridings, when he goeth to horseback . . . and by their blowings the household may follow in the countries. . . . The King will not that his minstrels be too presumptuous, to ask any rewards of the lords of his land'. Nevertheless entries in the accounts of the boroughs of Rye and Lydd and the other Cinque Ports, show that both the King's, the Queen's, and the Prince's minstrels did in fact earn money elsewhere than at court.

Every department of the household was ordered to the last detail, from the great offices down to the Chandlery, Ewery and Napery ('in covering of the board with wholesome, clean, and untouched cloths') to the Lavendry ('tenderly to wash and preserve diligently the stuff') the yeomen of which fetched the white, grey, and black soap from the Spicery, and the wood ash from the fires. 'And if there be a Queen in household, then there be women lavenders for the chamber, wardrobe, etc.' All this organisation was very necessary, for on great occasions more than two thousand persons were served at the King's board.

One of the most splendid ceremonies of the reign took place on 15th January, 1478, when the little Duke of York was married to Anne Mowbray, the only child and heiress of John Mowbray III, last Duke of Norfok of his line. This was the only one of the great marriages planned by Edward and Elizabeth for their children which was accomplished, but as neither the bridegroom nor the bride lived to grow up, it was no more than a flourish of trumpets. Anne Mowbray, who was six years old, was brought to Westminster Palace on the day before the wedding, and was led into the King's Great Chamber by Lord Rivers, where the whole court was gathered to receive her, and wine, sweetmeats, and spices were served. The next day she was led by the Earl of Lincoln and Earl Rivers in procession through the Queen's Chamber, and the King's Great Chamber, and the White Hall, into St Stephen's Chapel, attended by many ladies and gentlewomen. The chapel was hung with blue tapestry ornamented with gold *fleurs-de-lys*, and under a canopy of state sat the King and Queen, the Prince of Wales, the old Duchess of York, and the Princesses Elizabeth, Mary, and Cecily. The King gave the bride away; a largesse was thrown to the crowd out of bowls of gold and silver, and after the service spices and wine were served. Then the little bride, who was now entitled to be led by two royal dukes in place of the two earls, was conducted by the Duke of Gloucester and the Duke of Buckingham, the Queen's brother-in-law, to St Edward's Chamber, where the banquet was served. She was styled the Princess of the Feast, and she sat at the head of the first table, and gave a largesse to the heralds.

Some days later there was a great tournament, and the Princess of the Feast awarded the prizes, but as she was so young, she was assisted by the Princess Elizabeth and a council of ladies. These prizes were three golden initials; an A for Anne, set with a diamond; an E for Elizabeth, set with a ruby; and an M for Mowbray, set with an emerald. Lord Rivers cleverly combined his interest in religion and jousting, by appearing on the field dressed as a hermit all in white, bringing with him a tasteful hermitage of black velvet.

The royal family was much at Eltham during the last years of the reign, and Elizabeth's sixth daughter was born there in 1479, and named Katherine. Although the exact date of the Princess's birth is not known, an entry in the Wardrobe accounts of 3*d* for 500 nails spent ' about covering of the font at the christening of Lady Kateryn the King's daughter' appears in the year 1480. This small item in the accounts was probably overlooked for several months, and the Princess must have been born in the previous year, as her father was already negotiating for her marriage to the infant son of Ferdinand and Isabella of Spain in the month of August of the preceeding year. Possibly her godmother was the Queen's sister Katherine, the Duchess of Buckingham.

But if all that is known about this little princess's christening is that threepence was spent on nails, a detailed account of the christening of Elizabeth's youngest child has survived. For the last time Elizabeth 'took to her chamber', and her last child was born on 10th November, 1480, and christened the next day 'on the morn of St Martin's day, in the chapel at Eltham, by the Bishop of Chichester, in order as ensueth: First one hundred torches borne by knights, esquires, and other honest persons. The Lord Maltravers bearing the basin, having a towel about his neck. The Earl of Northumberland bearing a taper not lit. The Earl of Lincoln the salt. The canopy borne by four knights and a baron. My Lady Maltravers did bear a rich chrysom pinned over her left breast. The Countess of Richmond did bear the Princess. My Lord Marquis Dorset assisted her. My Lady the King's mother and my Lady Elizabeth were godmothers. The Bishop of Winchester was godfather.

'And in the time of the christening the officers-of-arms cast on their coats. And then were lit all the foresaid torches. Present these noblemen ensuing: The Duke of York, the Lord Hastings, the King's chamberlain, the Lord Stanley, steward of the

King's household, and many other estates. And when the said Princess was christened, a squire held the basins to the gossips . . . my Lady Maltravers was godmother to the Confirmation. And from thence she was borne before the high altar; and that solemnity done, she was borne eftsoons into a parclose [1] accompanied with the estates aforesaid. And the lord Saint James brought thither a spice plate: and at the said parclose the godfather and the godmother gave great gifts to the said princess. Which gifts were borne by knights and esquires before the said princess, turning to the Queen's chamber again, well accompanied as it appertaineth and after the custom of this realm.'

The custom of this realm was that an infant should be called by its name for the first time by its parents, and so the Princess Bridget was carried to Elizabeth's bedside, where Edward was also waiting, and together they named her and blessed her: the latest flower on the White Rose tree, and the last.

The closing years of Edward's reign were full of disappointment and vexation, yet the life of the Court seemed to grow only the more brilliant as the storm-clouds gathered on the horizon. The summer of 1480 was enlivened by a visit from Edward's favourite sister Margaret, the widow of Charles the Bold, who came to try and turn her brother from his alliance with France, and to press for the conclusion of the proposed match between

[1] A curtained part of the church.

her stepdaughter Mary's son, Philip, and the Princess Anne. Edward was in an awkward position; the darling scheme of his heart was the marriage of his eldest daughter to the Dauphin, and Burgundy and France were more deeply embroiled than ever; besides, if he broke with France, he must forgo his yearly tribute. After the death of Charles, Louis quietly annexed Burgundy, leaving only Flanders and the Low Countries to the young Duchess, whose sole hope of support lay in Edward.

Margaret was a true daughter of the House of York: beautiful, high-spirited, and scheming; and although Edward was determined to remain friends with Louis for his daughter's sake, when he saw his dearest sister once more, he was unable to resist her entreaties. A house called the Coldharbour in Thames Street was furnished for her use, and among entries in the Wardrobe Accounts may be noted two pieces of arras 'of the story of Paris and Elyn'; forty-seven yards of green sarsenet garnished with green ribbon for curtains, sheets, fustians, blankets, and 'great large feather beds'. Beds were works of art in the time of Edward IV, as witness this description of one, probably made for Margaret: 'Delivered for to make of a sperver of ray velvet of colours green, red, and white; the tester, ceiling, and vallance, of the same suit, lined with busk and fringed with fringe of silk of divers colours; with two side curtains and a foot curtain of sarsenet changeable.' A hundred servants were dressed in new 'jackets of woollen cloth of murrey and blue'. Sir Edward Woodville, one of the Queen's younger

ELIZABETH WOODVILLE, *circa* 1483

(STAINED GLASS WINDOW IN CANTERBURY CATHEDRAL)

brothers, went to Calais to fetch his sister-in-law in Edward's ship, the *Falcon*, and he and another knight were given 'a yard of velvet purple and a yard of blue velvet' to make themselves jackets with. At Gravesend the Duchess entered the King's barge, which was rowed by twenty-four men in 'jackets garnished with small roses embroidered'. The captain of the barge had a new coat of black camlet ornamented with a large rose; and a man named Peter Lumbard, embroiderer, was paid 'for eight great roses embroidered at fourpence each and for forty-eight small roses embroidered at a penny'. Edward gave his sister several horses and a magnificent pillion, harness of green velvet garnished with aglets of silver and gold, and bordered with spangles of silver, and headstalls and broad reins of crimson velvet. Her pillion was made of blue and purple cloth of gold, and 'fringed with blue and purple fringe, and fringe of Venice gold'.

As Margaret was young and handsome, she chose to ride on her new pillion when she left London after two months of festivity and negotiation. Together she and Edward rode through Kent and visited together the shrine of St Thomas at Canterbury. From Dover the *Falcon* bore her away from England and from Edward; she was happy in the knowledge that her mission was successful, nor did she realize that she would never see either again.

The dissensions of France and Burgundy were not the only problems, for Louis was busily at work making all the trouble for Edward that he could;

and he succeeded in spoiling the friendly relations between Scotland and England. Edward ceased his payments of the Princess Cecily's dowry, and preparations were begun for war. But Edward himself would never appear in a battlefield again, and all his energies were bent on arranging marriages for his children, while the Duke of Gloucester took command of the Army. The Prince of Wales was contracted to the daughter and heiress of the Duke of Brittany; the Princess Mary was contracted to the King of Denmark; while Louis was urged to pay the Princess Elizabeth's dowry and to name a date when she should be sent to France.

The future seemed full of hope for the children of Edward and Elizabeth, but one after another these hopes were shattered. First, the young Duchess of York died in the autumn of 1481, and was buried in the Chapel of St Erasmus which Elizabeth had founded in Westminster Abbey. Only a few months later the Princess Mary followed her. She died 'in the Tower of Greenwich' on 23rd May, 1482, at a moment of great anxiety for her father, when war with Scotland had just been declared, and Edward was on his way to the North. So the Prince of Wales was the chief mourner for his sister, who at the age of fifteen exchanged the crown of Denmark for a leaden coffin. The body was taken to Greenwich Church, where a dirge was sung, the Queen's sister Anne, Lady Grey de Ruthin, and many ladies attending. Later in the day the funeral train started towards Kingston-on-Thames, where it rested that night. Next morning the procession

178

started again with increased state, for a canopy was carried over the hearse by four gentlemen, and thirty poor men, holding lighted torches, walked beside it. At every village through which the procession passed, the people came out in mourning to pay their last respects to the princess. At Eton the mayor and aldermen of Windsor and others met the hearse, attired in white liveries, and carrying candles and torches. In St George's Chapel the Prince of Wales was waiting, 'and so she was buried by my lord her brother; and on the morrow she had her masses. On whose soul God have mercy.' Centuries later when the vault was opened, a lock of golden hair, stealing out through a chink in the decaying coffin, conjured up the pale image of a princess who might have been a Queen of Denmark.

The war with Scotland lasted till August, and was a triumph for the Duke of Gloucester, who took Berwick and advanced to Edinburgh. Edward himself took no part in it, for his lethargy increased as his health began to fail. In the autumn he made a pilgrimage to Walsingham, perhaps to pray for strength, but while Gloucester in the north grew every day stronger, Edward in the south grew daily weaker. Christmas came, and was celebrated with all the accustomed splendour; the King 'kept his estate all the whole feast in his Great Chamber and the Queen in her Chamber where were daily more than two thousand persons served'. The King could still excite admiration when he appeared in a dress of a new fashion with full hanging sleeves, like those of a monk. 'You might have seen in those days the royal Court presenting no other appearance than such as fully befits a most mighty kingdom, filled with riches and with people of almost all nations, and (apoint in which it excelled all others) boasting of those most sweet and beautiful children.'

The outward appearance of happiness was presented, but under the surface all the old jealousies were as active as ever. The court was divided into two rival parties, one headed by the Queen, consisting of her brothers and the two sons of her first marriage, of whom the elder, now the Marquis of Dorset, and about twenty-six years of age, was an added source of annoyance to the enemies of the Queen, because of the favour which the King showed to him. This party depended entirely on the King. The other party was headed by Lord Hastings; it included the Duke of Suffolk, the Duke of Buckingham, the Earl of Lincoln, and Lord Maltravers, all closely connected with the blood royal, besides many other noblemen who had never ceased to feel themselves slighted by the advancement of the Woodvilles. These men all looked to the Duke of Gloucester to support them in the future, and in the storm which gathered and broke upon them, some realized, when it was too late, that Gloucester looked to no one but himself.

Soon after Christmas Edward received news from France which staggered him. Disregarding his solemn promise, Louis betrothed the Dauphin to the daughter of Mary and Maximilian, and concluded a treaty of peace with Burgundy. To the disappointment which Edward felt because his eldest daughter would not be the Queen of France, was added the mortification of knowing that his foreign policy had been a complete failure. His spirit seemed to sink under the blow. Early in the new year Parliament was summoned and preparations were made for war, but it seems that the war was to be with Scotland rather than with France ; and this agreed with Gloucester's ambition, who did not care about his niece's future. The new Speaker was a special friend of his, and the Commons called the King's attention to the services which his brother had rendered in the late campaign against the Scots. Gloucester was granted the city and castle of Carlisle and the Wardenship of the West Marches for himself and his heirs male, besides palatine rights over certain lands beyond the Border if he could conquer them in the coming war. As one sun sank another rose, beside whose fierce light that of the Prince of Wales far away in Ludlow was but the feeble flicker of a candle.

But still, while the King lived (and no one yet supposed how soon he would die) the Woodvilles held the advantage; and now the gaps in the family, created by the death of Elizabeth's father and mother and third brother, were filled by her three remaining brothers, and by the two sons of her first marriage. The Marquis of Dorset was well on his way to becoming an important figure at this time, and his younger brother, Sir Richard Grey, was attached to the household of the Prince of Wales. Sir Edward

and Sir Richard Woodville were starting to carve
out careers for themselves, while Lionel became
Chancellor of Oxford University in 1479 and Bishop
of Salisbury three years later. In 1481 the Court was
at Woodstock, and old Bishop Waynflete, the
founder of Magdalen, called upon the King on
22nd September, and asked him to visit the new
college. Edward, in his amiable, impulsive way,
promised to come that very evening. He and
Elizabeth, with his mother, the Duchess of York,
and his sister, the Duchess of Suffolk, and a numerous train, arrived at St Giles's just after sunset; the
citizens turned out to greet them, carrying 'innumerable torches'. At the North Gate the royal
party was received by Lionel Woodville, and other
dignitaries, who escorted them to Magdalen, where
Waynflete received them. As there were several
bishops and noblemen in the King's train besides the
ladies, and as they all stayed the night in the college,
its resources must have been strained to the utmost;
but the University was grateful to the King for
sending his nephew, Edward de la Pole, there, and
with the Queen's brother for Chancellor, they hoped
to reap further benefits.

So when the year 1483 dawned, the Woodvilles
little thought how soon their gilded hopes would
vanish. On 2nd February, Candlemas day, the last
of the great ceremonial processions of the reign took
place, when Edward and Elizabeth walked from St
Stephen's Chapel into Westminster Hall, accompanied by the whole court. A few weeks later
Edward became alarmingly ill, and felt that he was

dying. Too late he realized the heritage of discord
which he was leaving to his eldest son; he summoned Hastings and Dorset to his bedside and
begged them to forget their enmity for his sake; and
they—moved, as many are in the presence of death,
to better things—joined their hands, although they
could not join their hearts. Knowing his brother's
strength without knowing his evil disposition,
Edward left the care of the new King to Gloucester;
he knew that Gloucester was the one man who was
capable of keeping order, but even so Edward can
hardly have closed his eyes in peace. He died on
9th April at the age of forty, and was buried in St
George's Chapel at Windsor with incredible pomp.

Where was in my life such one as I,
  While Lady Fortune with me had continuance?
Granted not she me to have victory,
  In England to reign, and to contribute France?
She took me by the hand and led me a dance,
  And with her sugared lips on me she smiled;
But, what for her dissembled countenance,
  I could not beware till I was beguiled:
Now from this world she hath me exiled;
  When I was loathest hence for to go,
And I am in age but, as who saith, a child,
  Et, ecce, nunc in pulvere dormio!

Where is now my conquest and victory?
  Where is my riches and my royal array?
Where be my coursers and my horses high?
  Where is my mirth, my solace, and my play?

As vanity, to naught all is wandered away.
  O lady Bess, long for me may ye call!
For now are we parted until doomsday;
  But love ye that Lord that is sovereign of all.
Where be my castles and buildings royal?
  But Windsor alone, now I have no mo,
And of Eton the prayers perpetual,
  Et, ecce, nunc in pulvere dormio![1]

---

[1] "Of the Death of the noble prince, King Edward the Fourth." John Skelton.

CHAPTER XI

DISASTER

"Small joy have I in being England's Queen."
King Richard III

DISASTER

WHATEVER may be thought of Edward's character, his personality was forceful, and his life was of great importance to his family. His death was a disaster to the Queen. To the grief of losing a husband who had been her constant friend, was added the certainty that now that he was no longer there to support her, there was no one else who would. She knew that in the eyes of those who hated her she was become no more than Elizabeth Woodville once again, and that the first action of her enemies would be to destroy the Woodvilles. From the moment of Edward's death, rumours began to circulate that his brother, and not his son, would be the next king, and if the common people thought so, Elizabeth must have had well grounded suspicions. The most vital thing was to get the young king to London as quickly and safely as possible, and to get him crowned, and at the first Council of the new reign Elizabeth impressed this upon the lords. She wanted the boy to come strongly armed. But Hastings and the Duke of Buckingham opposed the idea, for they feared that if Lord Rivers came to London with an army, they themselves might be the first to suffer. They persuaded her that there was nothing to fear, and that it would only cause needless alarm if forces were raised to accompany the king; and they pointed out that Gloucester himself had written her a conciliatory

letter professing his devotion to his nephew. So in
the end she gave way, and wrote to her brother
telling him to bring only 2,000 men with him.

The only man who could have saved the situation at this moment was Lord Rivers. If he had
hastened to London with the King all might have
been well; but he was far from being a man who
could pit himself against the Duke of Gloucester;
he lacked that spirit of ruthless determination, of
cruelty and cunning, which marked the man who
was soon to be Richard III. Doubtless he feared
Gloucester, but he hoped for the best. Besides,
Gloucester was making a show of loyalty to his
nephew; before he left York he took an oath of
allegiance to the new King, and he made all the
northern gentry do likewise. So just when prompt
action was needed, time was wasted. Not till a
fortnight after Edward's death did Lord Rivers
leave Ludlow with his precious charge; they proceeded in a leisurely manner towards London, and
they reached Stony Stratford just as Gloucester
reached Northampton. Stony Stratford!

Rivers and Sir Richard Grey, Elizabeth's second
son, went back to pay their respects to the Duke,
and they dined together in a friendly manner. Then
Buckingham arrived from London: no doubt he was
sent for. While Rivers and Grey were sleeping that
night, Gloucester and Buckingham were plotting.
Next morning Rivers and Grey were arrested, with
other gentlemen of the King's household, and sent
to the North to be imprisoned, while Gloucester
took possession of a weeping boy, and carried him

back to Northampton. It was the 30th April: the day on which Edward had arrived at Stony Stratford for his marriage to Elizabeth, nineteen years before.

Lord Rivers, who had no children of his own, had devoted himself to the education of the Prince whom he was never to see again. Caxton admired Lord Rivers as much for his character as for his services to literature, saying 'that he conceiveth well the mutability and unstableness of this worldly life, and that he desireth, with a great zeal and spiritual love, our ghostly help and perpetual salvation, and that we shall abhor and utterly forsake the abominable and damnable sins which commonly be used nowadays; as pride, perjury, terrible swearing, theft, murder, and other'. In fact, Lord Rivers and his sister, Elizabeth, had one fault in common, and for this they were both hated—they seized too gladly on what Fortune offered them; Elizabeth enjoyed being a queen, and Anthony enjoyed being a queen's brother. He did not live to see that the whole adventure had not been absolutely in vain.

Elizabeth was at Westminster when the news reached her, and her worst fears were fulfilled. Though she may not yet have credited Gloucester with a design to kill the King, some instinct told her to preserve the life of his brother. At midnight she left the Palace, and crossed the road to the postern gate in the wall of the Abbey precincts, taking her son the Duke of York and her daughters, 'and there lodged in the Abbot's place: she, and her children, and company, were registered as sanctuary

persons'. The last time that the children went
there, Cecily was the baby: now she was fourteen,
and Bridget was the baby: she was three years old.

Next morning, before it was light, a faithful
friend came to see her. This was Lord Chancellor
Rotheram, the Archbishop of York, who
courageously, but very foolishly, brought the Great
Seal with him, and gave it into her hands. It was
a sad sight that met his eyes in the torchlit gloom:

'The Queen sat alow on the rushes, all desolate
and dismayed, and all around her much heaviness,
rumble, haste, business, conveyance and carriage
of her stuff into sanctuary. Chests, coffers, packs,
fardels, trusses, all on men's backs, no man un-
occupied; some lading, some going, some dis-
charging, some coming for more: breaking down
the walls to bring in the next way. The Archbishop
comforted the Queen in the best way he could,
showing her that he trusted the matter was nothing
so sore as she took it for; and that he was put in
good hope and out of fear, by the message sent him
from my Lord Chamberlain. Ah, woe worth him,
quoth she, for he it is that laboureth to destroy me
and my blood. Madam, quoth he, be of good cheer,
for I assure you that if they crown any other king
than your son, whom they now have with them,
we shall, on the morrow, crown his brother, whom
you have here with you. And here is the great
Seal, which in likewise as your noble husband
delivered it unto me, so here I deliver it unto you;
and therewith he betook her the great Seal, and
departed home again, yet in the dawning of the

day. By which time he might, in his chamber window, see all the Thames full of boats of the Duke of Gloucester's servants, watching that no man should go to Sanctuary, nor none could pass unsearched.'

But the Archbishop was a man apparently more courageous by night than by day, and when the morning dawned, there also dawned upon him the fact that he had acted in a most unconstitutional manner, and he secretly sent for the Great Seal again.

The next day, the day which had been appointed for the Coronation, saw only the young King's arrival in the city. He was met at Hornsey by the Mayor and Aldermen, dressed in scarlet, and 500 citizens, dressed in violet, who accompanied him to the Bishop of London's palace at St Paul's, where he was lodged. The deferential attitude of his uncle was remarked and approved by all, for Gloucester was walking carefully, and he had some way to go yet before he could disclose his real intentions; the ground must be prepared. At a meeting of the Privy Council Gloucester was made Protector, and a Parliament was summoned; the date of the Coronation was fixed for 22nd June.

The thirteen year-old King did not at all like being at the Bishop of London's Palace, surrounded by strangers; and some members of the Council took pity on him, and suggested that he should go to Westminster, or to some place where he could have more freedom than in the City. Buckingham, probably at Gloucester's wish, suggested that he should be sent to the Tower in preparation for his coronation, and as this served the double purpose of lulling suspicion and keeping him safe, it was agreed upon. But what the Archbishop of York had said to the Queen was true: only a revolution could put Gloucester on the throne while both the young princes were alive; and so long as the Duke of York remained in sanctuary, it was useless for Gloucester to attempt to seize the crown. Some means must be found to get hold of the second heir.

Although Gloucester could count on the whole-hearted support of Buckingham, he was beginning to be doubtful about Hastings; and Hastings on his part was beginning to be very doubtful about Gloucester. It was one thing to get rid of the Woodvilles; but Hastings had no intention of doing anything which might hurt the son of Edward IV. He began to regret his hasty action in taking sides against the Queen, and he appears to have opened secret negotiations with her: he was observed to be holding mysterious conversations in St Paul's, with persons known to be connected with the Woodvilles. This was enough for the Protector: he determined to get rid of Lord Hastings. He devised a plan and carried it out swiftly. He divided the Council into two; in one half were the men whom he could trust to support him, and they were summoned to Westminster; the rest were to meet him at the Tower. 'Whereupon soon after . . . many Lords assembled in the Tower and there sat in council, devising the honourable solemnity of the king's coronation, of which the time appointed then so near approached, that the pageants and subtleties were in making day and night at Westminster, and much victual killed therefore, that afterwards was cast away. These lords so sitting together communing of this matter, the Protector came in among them, first about nine of the clock, saluting them courteously, and excusing himself that he had been from them so long, saying merely that he had been asleep that day. And after a little talking with them, he said unto the Bishop of Ely, My lord, you have very good strawberries at your garden in Holborn; I require you let us have a mess of them. Gladly, my lord, quoth he, would God I had some better thing as ready to your pleasure as that.

'And therewith all in haste he sent his servant for a mess of strawberries. The Protector set the lords fast in communing, and thereupon praying them to spare him a little while departed thence. And soon after one hour between ten and eleven he returned into the chamber among them, all changed, with a wonderful sour angry countenance, knitting the brows, frowning and frothing and gnawing on his lips and so sat down in his place, all the lords much dismayed and sore marvelling of this manner of sudden change, and what thing should him ail.' After scowling at them in silence for a while, he suddenly asked: 'What were they worthy to have that compass the destruction of me, being so near of blood unto the king and Protector of his royal person and his realm?' The lords were astonished, and Hastings replied 'that they were

worthy to be punished as heinous traitors whatsoever they were'. Upon this Gloucester said: 'That
is yonder sorceress my brother's wife and other with
her.' He then turned back his sleeve and pointed
to his withered arm,[1] which he declared was the
work of the Queen, in conspiracy 'with that other
witch of her council, Shore's wife'. Hastings did
not mind what accusations were levelled against
the Queen, but at the mention of Jane Shore he
changed countenance, for, since the King's death,
he had taken her under his protection.

Nevertheless Hastings endeavoured to calm the
Protector by appearing to agree with him, but in
vain. Gloucester 'clapped his fist upon the board a
great rap', and thereupon armed men rushed in
and seized Lord Hastings, who was immediately
hurried out to execution. 'It booted him not to
ask why, but heavily he took a priest at a venture,
and made a short shrift, for a longer would not
be suffered, the Protector made so much haste to
dinner. So was he brought forth into the green
beside the chapel within the Tower, and his head
laid down upon a long log of timber, that was there
for the building of the chapel, and there stricken
off.' The Archbishop of York and the Bishop of
Ely and the other members of the Council were
imprisoned in different parts of the Tower.

It now only remained to cover up this deed with a
semblance of justice, and to get hold of the little
Duke of York.

[1] In the portrait of Richard in the Rous Roll at the Herald's College,
his left arm appears to be smaller and shorter than his right.

The first was simple. Gloucester sent for the mayor and certain influential citizens, and, with Buckingham beside him, received them dressed in old armour, as though they had hastily snatched it up in a moment of self-defence. Gloucester explained that there had been a conspiracy by Lord Hastings to kill him. A proclamation was made describing the dangerous plot. 'Now was this proclamation made within two hours and it was so curiously indited, and so fair written in parchment, in so well a set hand, and therewith of itself so long a process, that every child might well perceive that it was prepared beforehand.'

One honourable man was gone, and two innocent boys must soon follow. Gloucester was determined to get hold of his younger nephew, but he was equally determined not to offend the Church or the people by taking him forcibly out of Sanctuary. He said: 'The privilege of that place, and other like, have been of long continued, and I am not he that would be about to break it. I will break no Sanctuary therefore.' But he cunningly suggested to the Council that because a Sanctuary was a place where criminals were immune from capture, it did not follow that a child, who had done no wrong, could claim the same protection; and he further said that it was sad for the young king to be all alone in the Tower, 'the prosperity whereof standeth not all in keeping from enemies or ill viand, but partly also in recreation and moderate pleasure: which he cannot in his tender youth take in company of ancient persons. . . . Wherefore with whom rather than with his own brother?' He sent Cardinal Bourchier, the Archbishop of Canterbury, the man who had crowned both Edward and Elizabeth, and who had been their friend for so many years, to persuade the Queen to give up the Duke of York. Bourchier took a number of lords with him, so that the Queen 'should perceive that this errand was not one man's mind'. He laid before her all the reasons against the boy's staying in the Sanctuary; that it gave rise to ugly rumours against the Protector, and disquieted the people; but particularly that the young king was anxious to have his brother with him. The Queen cleverly replied that it would be much better for both the boys if they were to be with their mother, and that the younger one was only just recovering from an illness 'and although there might be found other that would happily do their best unto him, yet is there none that knoweth better how to order him than I that so long hath kept him'.

The Archbishop agreed to this, but thought that it would be better if the Queen would either leave the sanctuary, or at least allow the Duke to leave it, adding that, at the time when her son the king kept 'his household in Wales, far out of your company, your Grace was well content therewith yourself. Not very well content, quoth the Queen, and yet the case is not like, for the one was then in health, and the other is now sick. . . . As for me, I purpose not as yet to depart hence. And as for this gentleman, my son, I mind that he shall be where I am, till I see further'. The Archbishop then said that the Protector feared lest the Queen should send the boy out of the country. 'Ay, sir, quoth the Queen, hath the Protector so tender zeal to him that he feareth nothing, but lest he should escape him. . . . In what place could I reckon him sure, if he be not sure in this the sanctuary, whereof there was never tyrant yet so devilish that durst presume to break.' She then touched on Gloucester's quibble that as the child was innocent of any crime he was not entitled to take sanctuary. 'Troweth the Protector (I pray God he may prove a protector) troweth he that I perceive not where unto his painted process draweth? It is not honourable that the Duke bide here: it were comfortable for them both that he were with his brother, because the King lacketh a playfellow . . . as though there could none be found to play with the King but if his brother, that hath no lust to play for sickness, come out of the sanctuary, out of his safeguard, to play with him. As though princes, as young as they be, could not play but with their peers, or children could not play but with their kindred. . . . I can no more, but whosoever he be that breaketh this holy sanctuary, I pray God shortly bring him need of sanctuary when he may not come to it; for taken out of sanctuary would I not that my mortal enemy were.'

The Cardinal, seeing that he could not move her with argument, offered to stake his own life upon the prince's safety. Elizabeth was in a fearful quandary, for she secretly feared that the Protector would take the child by force. When she heard the Cardinal make this solemn promise, which to his eternal shame he did not keep, 'she stood for a while in a great study,' thinking what was best to do; then she said: 'My lords . . . here is this gentleman, whom I doubt not I could keep safe if I would . . . here I deliver him, and his brother in him, into your hands, of whom I shall ask them both afore God and the world. Faithful ye be, that wot I well, and I know well you be wise. . . . But only one thing I beseech you, for the trust that his father put in you ever, and for the trust that I put in you now, that as far as you think that I fear too much, be you well aware that you fear not too little. And therewithall she said to the child, Farewell, my own sweet son, God send you good keeping. Let me kiss you once ere you go, for God knoweth when we shall kiss together again. And therewith she kissed him, and blessed him, turned her back and wept and went her way, leaving the child weeping as fast.'

On the 21st June one Simon Stallworth wrote to Sir William Storn: 'On Monday last was at Westminster great plenty of harnessed (armed) men. There was the deliverance of the Duke of York to my Lord Cardinal, my Lord Chancellor, and other many lords temporal. And with him met my Lord of Buckingham, in the midst of the hall of Westminster, and my Lord Protector receiving him, at the Star Chamber door, with many loving words: and so departed with my Lord Cardinal to the Tower, where he is, blessed be Jesu Mary.'

The fate of the young princes is one of those mysteries which may never be completely solved;

yet one significant and fearful fact remains. Sir Thomas More, writing in the next century, stated that the boys were smothered in their beds and their bodies buried 'at the stair foot, meetly deep in the ground, under a great heap of stones'. On the 17th July, 1674, when the staircase leading down from the chapel in the White Tower was being repaired, the skeletons of two boys were found.

More drew his information from Morton, Bishop of Ely, into whose household he was received as a young man: indeed it is thought by some that the narrative was written in Latin by Morton and only translated into English by More. Morton was actually present at the Council in the Tower after which Hastings was beheaded, and was later instrumental in bringing Henry VII to the throne. More's account of the Princes' murder is probably the weakest part of his narrative. He says: 'I shall rehearse you the dolorous end of those babes not after every way that I have heard it, but after that way that I have so heard, by such men and by such means, as me thinketh it were hard but it should be true.' Still, it must be remembered that whereas there were many witnesses of the interview between Elizabeth and Cardinal Bourchier, and also of the Council in the Tower, there can have been very few who were in the confidence of Richard III when he determined on the murder. According to More, Richard instructed Brackenbury, the Constable of the Tower, to do away with the boys, but as Brackenbury refused to be implicated in such a crime, he was ordered to give up the keys for one night to Sir

James Tyrell, who, with two men named Miles
Forest and John Dighton, then smothered the
princes in their beds. Tyrell and Dighton are said
to have confessed to the deed in the reign of
Henry VII, but nothing in writing has ever been
discovered, so that the method of the murder
remains a mystery.[1]

It was not in Edward's nature to be cruel to a
woman, but it was in Gloucester's; he persecuted
Elizabeth and he persecuted Jane Shore. Having
been since Edward's death the mistress of Hastings,
she naturally fell under the same suspicion for which
he was executed, and although it seems unlikely
that she was in league with the Queen, it is not
impossible that she was a go-between in any
plotting which there may have been. Whatever the
reason, she was arrested shortly after the Council
meeting in the Tower, and brought up before the
Bishop of London; she was accused of being a
harlot. This caused the citizens of London to laugh,
for Mistress Shore had been a harlot for so long that
it seemed rather late in the day to do anything about
it. She was condemned to do penance through the
streets of the city. But Jane was more than equal
to the ordeal, for when she appeared dressed only
in her shift and carrying a lighted candle, she looked
so lovely, 'so fair and lovely,' that all the people

[1] The quotations relating to the Council in the Tower and the scene
in the Sanctuary are taken from *The History of Richard III* by Sir Thomas
More. Bishop Morton heard with his own ears the words of Richard and
Hastings, and he was probably at pains to find out exactly what the Queen
said to the Archbishop. The interview in the Sanctuary must have been a
constant topic of conversation in London at the time, so that although
words put into the Queen's mouth were those of Sir Thomas More, the
thoughts behind them were her own.

RICHARD III

were moved to pity her; and they accused the Protector of spite, instead of being glad to 'see sin corrected'. So all that Gloucester got out of it was Jane Shore's worldly goods. She lived to a great age and died a poor woman; and when there was little food or firing, perhaps she warmed herself with the thought of her great days, when Edward loved her and men sought her help.

Having vented his spite on the late King's mistress, Gloucester proceeded to declare that the late King's wife was nothing more than a mistress. The story told by Stillington, the Bishop of Bath and Wells, was that Edward had promised marriage to a Lady Eleanor Butler, before he married Elizabeth; the Bishop had been sent to the Tower by Edward directly after Clarence's death for spreading this same story, which might then have helped Clarence to the throne, and he now hoped to avenge his disgrace on Edward's family. As Edward and Elizabeth had been married for eighteen years without any mention being made of Lady Eleanor Butler, it seemed as late in the day to bring the matter up as it was to tell people that Jane Shore's private life was irregular. But Richard's wizened face made quite as much impression on the citizens of London as Edward's handsome one had done. Richard's eyes ' whirled about' and his hand was ever on his dagger: Edward's eyes were dazzling and his hand was graciously waved to the admiring crowd: each in his own way fascinated his subjects, and one was loved and the other was feared. Doctor Shaw, the brother of the Mayor of London, was put up to preach a sermon on Sunday, 22nd June, and he took for his text: 'Bastard slips shall not take deep root.' 'He showed openly that the children of King Edward IV were not legitimate nor rightful inheritors of the crown'; nor was this all, for an old calumny against Richard's own mother was revived: the story that Edward was not the son of the Duke of York, but of a handsome archer. This strange story had also been used by Clarence in the past, for it seemed that the sons of the House of York would stick at nothing where their ambition was involved.

The mind of the people was now prepared for what was coming, and next day a Grand Council was held at St Paul's, when the marriage of Edward was declared illegal, because the banns had not been called; because it had taken place in a 'profane' place—a private chamber; and because the bridegroom already had a wife living at the time. Once again the accusations of sorcery and witchcraft were brought against Elizabeth and her mother, as the means whereby they had procured the marriage, and then Richard was asked to accept the crown. He was prayed to accept it, and, clever actor that he was, he appeared to hesitate; then he graciously gave way.

One blow after another fell upon Elizabeth during these terrible weeks. It was not enough that her son was deposed and that her younger son was taken away from her; that her marriage was declared no marriage, and that her children were called bastards. One more disaster was added to these when her brother Anthony, and her son Sir Richard Grey, were executed at Pontefract, together with Vaughan and Haute, two faithful friends. When Elizabeth heard the news she gave herself up to despair. Her agony of mind must have been increased by living so close to the scene of her former happiness; she could not help hearing the clatter and clamour when Richard came to Westminster to take his seat upon the throne which should have belonged to her son; she heard the bells ringing for the coronation of the new king: the Te Deum which was sung, and the cries of 'King Richard! King Richard!' which should have been acclamations for her son. She fell ill with too much grief.

Elizabeth still had a few friends left, though very few. The best of these was John Morton, Bishop of Ely, who unlike the treacherous Archbishop Bourchier, had not forgotten what he owed to his late sovereign. Lionel, and Edward, and Richard Woodville, were still alive, and so was her eldest son, the Marquis of Dorset, and her brother-in-law, the Duke of Buckingham, who all this time had been with Richard, but who now turned against him and raised a rebellion.

The original plan was undoubtedly to restore Edward V, but another one was soon substituted, when it became known that the Princes were dead; for secretly as the deed was done, the truth leaked out.

'Foul deeds will rise,
  Though all the world o'erwhelm them, to men's
    eyes.'

The plan which these men now adopted originated with the Bishop of Ely, and it shows that it was generally believed that the Princes were no longer alive.

Ever since the battle of Tewkesbury, there had been living in Brittany a young man whose claim to be the last heir of Lancaster caused him to be looked upon with great suspicion by the House of York. His claim was slender indeed, but if York could claim the throne through Anne Mortimer, Henry Tudor could claim it through his mother, Margaret Beaufort, for she was the great-granddaughter of John of Gaunt. He might just as well have claimed the throne of France, since he was the grandson of that Katharine who had disgraced herself by marrying the 'goodly gentleman and beautiful person called Owen Tudor'; but in the absence of any more important Lancastrian heirs, his mother, the Lady Margaret, at least, considered that he was entitled to the throne of England. The new plan was to marry him to the Princess Elizabeth, and in the first place it was necessary to communicate with her mother.

It was very difficult to get into the sanctuary at Westminster, as Richard kept a guard upon the Precincts, but the Lady Margaret, who can hardly have cared much for Elizabeth Woodville up till now, suddenly expressed great anxiety for her health, and sent her physician, a man named Lewis, to attend upon Elizabeth. Under cover of this visit, Elizabeth gave her consent to the scheme, and sent word that all her friends were to follow the Duke of Buckingham. But the hopes thus raised were soon dashed, for the rising was a total failure: the Duke of Buckingham was taken and executed, and the Bishop of Ely and the Marquis of Dorset fled out of the country.

'Hope deferred maketh the heart sick,' and Elizabeth's heart was very sick. Her position was terrible. She had no money, and no means of getting any; all her property was confiscated by the new King, and she could only live on the charity of the Abbot of Westminster, who was probably as frightened of Richard as everyone else, and beginning to be embarrassed by the presence of the Queen. Richard for his part was determined to get Elizabeth and her daughters out of the sanctuary into some place where he could watch them more closely, his one fear being lest the Princesses should escape out of the country; for although the common people might be hoodwinked about the validity of Edward's marriage, Richard knew well enough that the Princess Elizabeth was the true heir to the throne. It became clear to the Queen that she could not spend all the rest of her life within the walls of Westminster Abbey precincts, less still ought her daughters to do so, and as Richard was a cunning flatterer, he now tried cajolements in place of threats. With fair promises at last he got Elizabeth out, though not on his promise, which she could not trust, but after he had sworn a solemn oath before a public assembly:

'I, Richard, by the Grace of God King of England and of France and Lord of Ireland, in the presence of you, my lords spiritual and temporal and you Mayor and Aldermen of my City of London, promise and swear verbo regio upon these holy Evangels of God by me personally touched, that if the daughters of dame Elizabeth Gray, late calling herself Queen of England, that is to wit Elizabeth, Cecily, Anne, Katharine, and Bridget, will come unto me out of the Sanctuary of Westminster, and be guided, ruled and demeaned after me, then I shall see that they shall be in surety of their lives, and also not suffer any manner of hurt by any manner person or persons to be done, by way of ravishment or defiling contrary to their wills, nor them or any of them imprisoned within the Tower of London or other prison; but that I shall put them in honest places of good name and fame, and them honestly and courteously shall see to be founden and entreated, and to have all things requisite and necessary for their exhibition and findings as my kinswomen; and that I shall marry such of them as be marriageable to gentlemen born, and every of them give in marriage lands and tenements to the yearly value of two hundred marks for the term of their lives; and in likewise to the other daughters when they come to lawful age of marriage if they live. And such gentlemen as shall happen to marry with them I shall straitly charge, from time to time, lovingly to love and entreat them as their wives and my kinswomen, as they will avoid and eschew my displeasure.

'And over this, that I shall yearly from henceforth content and pay, or cause to be contented or

paid, for the exhibition and finding of the said dame
Elizabeth Gray during her natural life, at four
terms of the year, that is to wit at Pasche, Mid-
summer, Michaelmas, and Christmas, to John
Nesfield, one of the squires of my body, for his
finding to attend upon her, the sum of seven hundred
marks of lawful money of England, by even portions; and moreover I promise to them that if any
surmise or evil report be made to me of them, or
any of them, by any person or persons, that then
I shall not give thereto faith nor credence, nor therefore put them to any manner punishment, before
that they or any of them so accused may be at their
lawful defence and answer. In witness whereof,
to this writing of my oath and promise aforesaid
in your said presences made I have set my sign
manual, the first day of March, the first year of my
reign.'[1]

This man Nesfield had been in charge of the
soldiers who guarded the sanctuary. He must have
been one of Richard's most trusted servants, and he
now became, to all intents and purposes, Elizabeth's
gaoler. The sad little company left the precincts
and crossed the road; they entered the palace with
fear in their hearts, not trusting even an oath. The
one thing which mattered was to gain time. Henry
Tudor was still safe in Brittany, and three months
before, in Rennes Cathedral, he had sworn an oath
to marry the Princess Elizabeth. Her mother set
herself to match cunning with cunning, and fair
words with words as fair.

[1] Ellis's *Original Letters*, second series, vol. i.

In April Richard tasted something of the grief which he had inflicted on Elizabeth, when his only son, whom he had lately created Prince of Wales, died. The new Queen, Anne Neville, was slowly dying, and never likely to have another child. A new idea came into Richard's mind; he would marry the Princess Elizabeth himself, and so prevent Henry Tudor from doing so.

It was said in later years that Elizabeth Woodville encouraged this scheme, but this can only have been a blind to flatter her enemy. She must have realised that a Papal dispensation for such an incestuous marriage would be very difficult to obtain. When the news of Richard's intended infamy became known, certain gentlemen took it upon themselves to tell him that the people of England would never countenance it, and he was obliged to yield. The Princess, who had latterly been treated with great favour, and dressed in garments befitting a queen, was sent away to Yorkshire, where she was kept closely guarded in the castle of Sheriff Hutton, in company with a boy who also had more right to the throne than Richard—the son of Clarence.

It is difficult to imagine a situation more forlorn than Elizabeth's was at this time. She had to mourn a husband dead, a son and brother executed, and two sons murdered; she saw her daughters bastardized, and her marriage dishonoured; she was deprived of her liberty, and separated from her eldest daughter; she was dependent for everything on the man who had caused all her griefs, except her husband's death. There was nothing to comfort her: no change of scene, no fresh interest. To a woman who had been for nearly twenty years the mistress of Edward's splendid court, constantly moving from one palace to another, entertained, courted, and admired, the days must now have passed in a dreariness that was little better than death.

Yet six months later Henry Tudor landed in England: the battle of Bosworth was fought, and Richard's life was ended.

CHAPTER XII

LAST YEARS OF ELIZABETH

Somewhat musing
 And more mourning,
In remembering
 The unsteadfastness,
This world being
Of such wheeling,
 What may I guess

Methinks truly
Bounden am I,
And this greatly,
 To be content;
Seeing plainly
That fortune doth wry
All contrary
 From mine intent.

Anthony Woodville
(lines composed the night before his execution)

CHAPTER XII
LAST YEARS OF ELIZABETH

EDWARD was gone: the Rose of Rouen. Richard was gone: the 'bottled spider'. Now came a man very different from either. The flamboyant personalities of Henry Tudor's two predecessors seem all the more dramatic beside his uninspiring figure: wise, quiet, and cautious, he was a great king, although he was not a great man.

To Elizabeth Woodville and her children his victory at Bosworth meant everything, for their whole future depended on him; and although Henry was not a generous man his behaviour to them was honourable, even if it was not princely. Directly after his accession, the Princess Elizabeth was released from the Castle at Sheriff Hutton, and restored to her mother. Her progress to London was triumphal, for the people flocked to see the beautiful girl who was to be their queen. She was nineteen years old, tall and stately, with her mother's golden hair, and her father's dark eyes; her expression, which proceeded from the goodness of her heart, was of the 'most enchanting sweetness'. Doubtless they hoped that Henry would immediately fulfil his promise to marry the Princess, so that the White and the Red Rose might be crowned together. But Henry, like William of Orange later, was far from wishing to reign by right of his wife, and he was very anxious to get his own claims thoroughly established without any assistance from the House of York. His

213

own coronation was announced: it came, and passed, and still he made no arrangements for his wedding; and when Parliament met he even secured the crown to his heirs, without binding himself to marry the Princess. However, a month later, when the same Parliament was prorogued, the Speaker presented a petition from the Commons, requesting the King to marry the Lady Elizabeth of York; and to this the King gave his gracious assent.

But though Henry temporised over his marriage, he did not forget what he owed to Elizabeth Woodville. One of his first acts after his accession was to restore her to her rightful rank as the widow of a king, and to grant her for life six manors in Essex, besides an annual income of £102 to be paid from the revenues of the city of Bristol; and though nothing could wipe out the memory of Richard's cruelty, there was some satisfaction in knowing that the Parliamentary rolls, which embodied her own and her daughters' disgrace, were to be burnt, because 'from their falseness and shamefulness, they were only deserving of utter oblivion'.

For a time Elizabeth returned to public life. On 18th January, 1486, she had the satisfaction of seeing her eldest daughter married to the King at Westminster, and 'by reason of this marriage peace was thought to descend out of heaven into England'. But this was not so, for in the spring there was a rising in Yorkshire, and Henry, who was already making a Royal Progress, was obliged to go there; he was away from his young wife for six months. She passed the summer at Winchester with her mother and her sisters and the King's mother, peacefully awaiting the birth of a child. Winchester was chosen by Henry as the place where his heir should be born, because of its association with King Arthur, a supposed ancestor of the Tudors. In September, Henry arrived in the city only just in time, for his eldest son was born three days later, and some weeks sooner than was expected. So Elizabeth Woodville became the grandmother of a prince, and the last triumph of her life came when she was chosen to be his godmother, rather than the King's mother, the Lady Margaret. Her second daughter, the Princess Cecily, carried the child to the font, and Elizabeth gave her godson a covered cup of gold.

For a while after this Elizabeth fell under the King's displeasure, and was obliged to retire to the Abbey of Bermondsey; the lands which had been given her were confiscated and she was granted instead the paltry sum of four hundred marks a year. The reason for this action was not publicly stated, but the inference was that she was connected with the conspiracy which put forward a youth named Lambert Simnel as one of the Princes who were murdered in the Tower. Any gleam of hope which reached her that either of her sons was still alive could not fail to be of lively interest to Elizabeth, and she may have been indiscreet in showing that she hoped it must be true; but as the supposed identity of Simnel was soon changed by his supporters to that of the young Earl of Warwick, Clarence's only surviving son, whom Elizabeth well knew was imprisoned in the Tower, she cannot have been very deeply implicated in the matter. However, Henry was in such terror of a rising on the behalf of the Yorkists, that his suspicions of his mother-in-law were probably exaggerated; but he took the opportunity of showing her clearly what the effect of any plotting would be.

It can hardly be supposed that Elizabeth was very happy at this time: it could not now come easily to her to take the second place. Nor did she even take the second place, for though her rank entitled her to take precedence over the King's mother, it was the Lady Margaret, that vaunted paragon of women, who ruled the royal household. The new Queen was placid and pliable, devoted to her husband and her mother-in-law, who took care to be always about her with wise counsel. Elizabeth must have felt jealous of this rival influence over her daughter, and probably it was more peaceful at court when she was not there. She was not present at her daughter's coronation and she only saw from afar the procession of boats upon the Thames when the new Queen came up from Greenwich to the Tower.

Whatever the cause of Elizabeth's exile, it did not last long, for at the very time of the coronation Henry was arranging another marriage for his mother-in-law. Had it been accomplished, Elizabeth's life-story would have been even more astonishing than it already was, for then she would have been not only Queen of England, but also of Scotland. Henry, who wished for friendly relations with Scotland, proposed no less than three marriages between the two royal families: Elizabeth should marry James III, a widower some fifteen years younger than herself; his eldest son should marry one of her daughters, 'which liketh best to both Kings', and the Princess Katharine should marry the King of Scotland's second son. This wholesale dumping of his wife's relations on James would seem to argue that Henry was not altogether deficient in humour. If the marriages had taken place, Elizabeth would soon have found herself a Queen-Dowager once again, for it was ever a precarious position to be King of Scotland, and James III was murdered shortly afterwards, in civil war with his own son. This son, when he later became King, married, not a daughter of Elizabeth's, but her granddaughter, Margaret.

In the autumn of 1489 Henry's second child was born, and Elizabeth assisted at the ceremony when her daughter 'took to her chamber'.

'Allhallows-eve the Queen took to her chamber at Westminster royally accompanied; that is to say, with my lady the Queen's mother, the Duchess of Norfolk, and many other going before her, and besides greater part of the nobles of the realm assembled at Westminster at the Parliament. She was led by the Earl of Oxford and the Earl of Derby. The reverend father in God, the Bishop of Exeter, said mass in his pontificals, and the Earl of Salisbury held the towels when the Queen received the Host, and the corners of the towels were golden. . . . When she arrived at her great chamber she tarried in the ante-room before it, and stood under her cloth of estate;

then was ordained a voide of refreshments. That done, the Queen's chamberlain, Sir Richard Pole, in very good words, desired in the Queen's name all her people to pray that God would send her a good hour, and so she entered into her chamber which was hanged and ceiled with blue cloth of arras.'

From this moment no one but women ought to have come near the Queen, but for once this rule was set aside when one of those relatives from Luxembourg, once so sought-after by her father, arrived on an embassy from France. Almost for the last time Queen Elizabeth Woodville was her old proud self when she received her princely relative in state and insisted on taking him to see her daughter, the Queen of England. She was not old yet, but she was ageing; the century was drawing to a close, and with it her life was ending. One more grandson was born, a robustious boy who was called Henry; but when, less than a year later, a second daughter was born, she could only be named in memory of her grandmother, for Elizabeth Woodville was dead.

Elizabeth died in Bermondsey Abbey, on the Friday before Whit Sunday, in the year 1492, at the age of fifty-five. Her three youngest daughters were with her at the last. Two years previously Henry granted her an annuity of four hundred pounds, so that she was not harassed for money at the end of her life, particularly as she could claim free hospitality from the Abbey, since her husband had been a descendant of the founder. On the other hand, as her income was only for life, she had no lands which she could leave to her daughters. Gone were the goods and chattels, the arrases and tapestries, the plate and jewels, which Edward left to her; nothing remained but such few personal belongings as were necessary to her comfort. Her will, which she dictated on her death-bed, is short and simple; indeed the two or three letters of hers which have survived show that she could express herself clearly and well, without the tiresome repetition which was used by most people at the time.[1]

'In the name of God, &c., 10th April, 1492, I, Elizabeth, by the grace of God queen of England, late wife to the most victorious prince of blessed memory, Edward IV. Item. I bequeath my body to be buried with the body of my lord at Windsor, without pompous interring or costly expenses done thereabout. Item. Whereas I have no worldly goods to do the queen's grace, my dearest daughter, a pleasure with, neither to reward any of my children according to my heart and mind, I beseech God Almighty to bless her grace, with all her noble issue; and, with as good a heart and mind as may be, I give her grace my blessing, and all the aforesaid my children. Item. I will that such small stuff and goods that I have be disposed truly in the contentation of my debts, and for the health of my soul, as far as they will extend. Item. That if any of my blood will to have any of my said stuff, to me pertaining, I will they have the preferment before all others. And of this my present testament I make and ordain my executors—that is to say, John Ingilby, prior of the

[1] See Appendix 5. Letter of Elizabeth Woodville to Sir William Stonor.

Charterhouse of Shene, William Sutton and Thomas Brent, doctors. And I beseech my said dearest daughter, the queen's grace, and my son, Thomas marquis of Dorset, to put their good wills and help for the performance of this my testament. In witness whereof to this my testament, these witnesses—John, abbot of Bermondsey, and Benedict Cun, doctor of physic.'

The Queen's funeral was neither pompous nor costly; indeed it was so shabby that it gave offence to many who felt that the family of York had been tricked out of their heritage by Henry Tudor. Henry himself was far too stingy to waste good money on lavish obsequies for his mother-in-law; and the young Queen had taken to her chamber in anticipation of the birth of her fourth child; so that she was unable to see that even the necessary formalities were decently carried out. Those who attended were those who felt a real affection for the dead woman: her younger daughters, a few friends, and, most touching of all, Mistress Grace, a bastard daughter of Edward's who floats into history upon the funeral barge of a queen, and who was the only gentlewoman to accompany the body from Bermondsey to Windsor. Surely this shows a generous spirit in Elizabeth, when it can be said of her that she inspired devotion in one whom she had little reason to befriend, and that when she fell on evil days, she did not forget a woman whom perhaps no one else would have remembered.

'On Whit-Sunday, the queen-dowager's corpse

was conveyed by water to Windsor, and there privily, through the little park, conducted into the castle, without any ringing of bells or receiving of the dean, but only accompanied by the prior of the Charterhouse, and Dr. Brent, Mr. Haute, and mistress Grace (a bastard daughter of king Edward IV), and no other gentlewoman; and, as it was told to me, the priest of the college received her in the castle and so privily, about eleven of the clock, she was buried, without any solemn dirge done for her obit. On the morn thither came Audley, bishop of Rochester, to do the office, but that day nothing was done solemnly for her; saving also a hearse, such as they use for the common people, with wooden candlesticks about it, and a black (pall) of cloth of gold on it, four candlesticks of silver gilt, every one having a taper of no great weight. On the Tuesday hither came, by water, king Edward's three daughters, the Lady Anne, the lady Katherine, and the lady Bridget from Dartford, accompanied by the marchioness of Dorset; lady Herbert, niece to the queen; dame Katherine Gray; dame Guildford: their gentlewomen walked behind the three daughters of the dead. Also that Tuesday came the marquis of Dorset, son to the queen, the earl of Essex, her brother-in-law; and the viscount Welles, her son-in-law. And that night began the dirge. But neither at the dirge were the twelve poor men clad in black, but a dozen divers old men, and they held old torches and torches' ends. And the next morning one of the canons, called Master Vaughan, sang Our Lady mass, at which the lord Dorset offered a piece of gold; he kneeled at the hearse-head. The ladies came not to the mass of requiem, and the lords sat about in the quire. My lady Anne came to offer the mass-penny, and her officers-at-arms went before her: she offered the penny at the head of the queen, wherefore she had the carpet and the cushion. And the viscount Welles took his (wife's) offering, and dame Katherine Gray bare the lady Anne's train: every one of the king's daughters offered. The marquis of Dorset offered a piece of gold, and all the lords at their pleasure; the poor knights of Windsor, dean, canons, yeomen, and officers-at-arms, all offered: and after mass, the lord marquess paid the cost of the funeral.'

Historians are fond of saying that Edward was a bad man, cruel, licentious, and treacherous, and that Elizabeth was an ambitious woman, proud, capricious, self-seeking. While some will extenuate Edward's faults by pointing to his courage on the battle-field, his generosity to his friends, and his gift for organization, few if any have tried to find a good word for Elizabeth. Yet in one thing these two gave an example to their people: that was in family affection. The almost total want of domestic feeling at the time is so marked that it inspires abhorrence. 'There are few periods in our annals from which the mind turns with such weariness and disgust as from the Wars of the Roses.'[1] It is not only the battles and the cruelty, but the baseness of the national character which inspires this feeling of revulsion.

[1] J. R. Green, *A Short History of the English People.*

Foreigners were more than surprised at 'the cold-heartedness of parents towards their children, the want of tenderness in husbands towards their wives, the mercenary way in which marriages were contracted by parents or guardians for the young people under their charge'.[1] If no one will deny that Edward and Elizabeth were mercenary in the matter of the marriages of their relations and children, let it at least be said of Edward that he married for love, and of them both that they lived in mutual affection and that they loved their children.

If there was one thing which could comfort the dying thoughts of Elizabeth, it was her eldest daughter's happiness; she alone of the children fulfilled a destiny such as her parents devised for her. She was safely provided for, and honourably situated; and if she was not completely happy with her cold-hearted husband, she had other sources of satisfaction in her children and in the love of her people. Her death, at the age of thirty-eight, was universally mourned, and was perhaps most keenly felt by her sisters, for to them she was a second mother. Because of Henry's avarice, his wife was kept very short of money, but she was always ready to help the sisters who were less fortunate than herself.

After a few half-hearted attempts to find husbands for his sisters-in-law among the lesser princes of Europe, Henry fell back on what was probably a fixed intention of marrying them to people of less importance. In his heart there lingered an inborn hatred of the House of York, and a rising on its

[1] James Gairdner, Introduction to *The Paston Letters*.

behalf was what he most dreaded; to give any foreign
prince the shadow of a right to claim the throne of
England was the last thing which Henry wanted,
and the necessity which would have arisen of giving
handsome dowries to the princesses was an equally
potent reason against foreign alliances.

Cecily, 'not so fortunate as fair,' married first; indeed she married before her mother's death. Perhaps something of her father's spirit moved her to
marry for love, since her husband John, Viscount
Wells, was hardly a good enough match for the
daughter of the King of England.

Maybe Cecily was tired of waiting for Henry to do
something for her, and decided to take the future into
her own hands; she chose a husband twenty years
older than herself, who was the half-brother of the
Lady Margaret, the King's mother. The wedding, if
not actually secret, was celebrated very quietly, and
no account of it, not even the date, has survived; but
it must have taken place before 1487, as Lord and
Lady Wells were present at the Christmas festivities
at Greenwich Palace in that year. After this Cecily
is lost sight of for a while, and she may have retired
from the court and lived on her husband's estates.
This would explain why she was not at her mother's
funeral, where she was represented by Lord Wells, as
only three days elapsed between the death and the
funeral and the news may not have reached her in
time. She had two daughters, but one of these was
already dead when Lord Wells died in 1498. He was
buried in Westminster Abbey with all the fearful
pageantry associated with the funerals of the nobility

at the time; but an indication that Cecily was not wealthy is given by the fact that she did not provide mourning garments for the guests. Soon after this her second child also died, so that she was left a sorrowful woman at the age of thirty. She probably returned to the court for the next few years, as she was present at the wedding of Prince Arthur and Catherine of Aragon in 1501, when she carried the bride's train, and her fair beauty must have contrasted noticeably with the plain face and dark complexion of the Spanish princess. Two years later she and her sisters lost their best friend, when the Queen died.

Cecily married again soon afterwards a gentleman of obscure birth, opprobiously referred to by old-time genealogists as 'one, Kyme of Lincolnshire', and she lived 'not in great wealth' in the Isle of Wight. It can be imagined that Henry, who covered up the doubtful spots in his own genealogy by laying stress on his imaginary descent from King Arthur, did not recognise 'one, Kyme of Lincolnshire', as a brother-in-law, and Cecily was forgotten; the two children of the marriage were never recognized by their haughty relatives. So Cecily faded away, and died, not long afterwards, at the age of thirty-eight. When her nephew, Henry VIII, proceeded to the dissolution of the Monasteries, he destroyed the Abbey of Quarre, where his aunt lay buried, so that not even a monument of stone remained to show where the fairest of all Edward's fair daughters rested. Perhaps Lord Wells and Kyme of Lincolnshire were kind husbands, who brought her more happiness than the crown of Scotland would have done, but there is something faintly sad about the life of this princess, for a beauty so remarkable as to call forth praise from the soulless chroniclers of the time, deserved some better fate than obscurity and an early death.

The Princess Anne, who was seventeen when her mother died, took the place of Cecily at court; but when she married, she too lived in comparative obscurity. Her husband was Thomas, Lord Howard, the son of the Earl of Surrey and the grandson of that pushing and energetic Sir John Howard who had been so assiduous in seeking the favour of Elizabeth Woodville when she became Queen. Sir John became Lord Howard in Edward's reign, and was created Duke of Norfolk by Richard; he was killed at Bosworth, and as his estates were confiscated by Henry VII, the family were no longer rich. However, his son, the Earl of Surrey, Anne's father-in-law, earned Henry's trust and became one of the important figures of the time. Anne must have been very delicate; she had several children, but these all died in infancy, and she herself died at thirty-seven or thirty-eight, an age which seemed fatal to these sisters. She was buried at Thetford, but like Cecily, her rest was disturbed by her nephew Henry. Her husband sought permission from the King to convert the priory into a 'very honest parish church'; but in vain. So her monument was transferred to Framlingham, where her recumbent effigy may still be seen, lying on the right of her husband, in compliment to her royal birth. Lord Howard became in time the third Duke of Norfolk, the uncle of Anne Boleyn and Katherine Howard, and the father, by his second wife, of the celebrated soldier-poet Henry, Earl of Surrey. He was a very important personage in the reign of Henry VIII, but his character was detestable, and the Princess Anne can hardly have been happy with him.

The Princess Katherine, who was thirteen years old when her mother died, soon married Lord William Courtenay, son and heir of the Earl of Devon. Katherine was the only one of her sisters who lived on into middle age: 'long time she tossed in either fortune, some time in adversity, some time in wealth.' In the early years of her marriage, Katherine lived in affluence on her husband's estates in Devonshire. The young couple were present at the marriage of Prince Arthur to Catherine of Aragon when Lord Courtenay distinguished himself at the ensuing tournament, and they were again present at court in the following year, when the Princess Margaret was betrothed to James IV of Scotland. But soon after this a change occurred in Katherine's fortunes, for her husband fell under suspicion of being concerned with Edmund de la Pole [1] in treasonable designs against the King; he was attainted and sent to the Tower. For a while Katherine and her three children were supported by the Queen, and when she died Katherine and Anne were the chief mourners at their sister's funeral; but afterwards Katherine lived in complete obscurity till the end of her brother-in-law's reign.

The accession of her nephew brought a return to prosperity; Lord Courtenay was released from the

---

[1] The son of Edward IV's sister, the Duchess of Suffolk.

Tower, after what was probably an unjust imprisonment of seven years, and on the birth of a son to the new Queen Catherine, Lady Courtenay was chosen to be the sole godmother. For two years they lived at court and enjoyed the favour of the King, their nephew; but when Lord Courtenay died, Katherine took a vow of chastity, and retired to her estates in Devonshire, where she lived in considerable state for the rest of her life. The attainder on her husband was reversed just before his death and the earldom of Devon restored to him, and his widow's broad seal bore the inscription 'Katherine, Countess of Devon, daughter, sister, and aunt of kings' with the royal arms of England quartered with those of Ulster and Mortimer, impaling the Courtenay arms.

So at least Katherine was more prosperous than her sisters; but her misfortunes were not at an end. She had already lost one of her sons in childhood, and when her only daughter, the Lady Margaret Courtenay, was fourteen years old, she died suddenly as the result of being choked by a fish-bone. Katherine herself died in 1527 at the age of forty-nine, and her funeral, which was celebrated with royal honours, was superintended by Norroy, king-of-arms. Two years before her death she had the satisfaction of seeing her son created Marquis of Exeter, and of supposing that his future was secured. Yet the fate of her son and grandson was as disastrous as that of so many of her near relatives. Her son was executed in 1539 on suspicion of being connected with Cardinal Pole in treasonable activities, while her grandson, a boy of twelve at the time of his father's death, was sent to the Tower, where he remained for many years. Eventually he too incurred the displeasure of his cousin, Queen Mary, and was banished. He died in Italy in 1556 at the age of twenty-nine, without leaving any children.

The Princess Bridget appears to have been sent at a very early age to a convent of close nuns at Dartford in Kent. She may have been extremely delicate, perhaps even feeble-minded, for it seems curious for so young a child to be immured in a convent. She came out only once in her life, when she was twelve years old, to visit her mother's death-bed and to attend the funeral. Soon afterwards she took the veil. She never gained a higher rank than that of an ordinary nun, and she died probably before the year 1513, as Sir Thomas More, who wrote his history of Richard III about that time, in enumerating the daughters of Edward IV says of the Lady Catherine only that 'yet she liveth'. Certain sums of money are mentioned in the accounts of Elizabeth of York as paid to the Abbess of Dartford 'towards the charges of my Lady Bridget'. She was buried within the priory church, but her tomb suffered the same fate as that of her sister Cecily. Henry VIII converted the priory into a residence, and Anne of Cleves lived in it for a time after she was separated from him; but only a fragment of the building now remains, hemmed in by factories and modern buildings.

The only surviving son of Elizabeth Woodville, Thomas Grey, Marquis of Dorset, was in fairly high favour with Henry VII, although he spent a short

time in the Tower on some suspicion of being implicated in the Lambert Simnel rising in 1487; but as
he received a gold ring worth £100 from the King in
1492, all was apparently forgiven and forgotten.
Three years later there is an entry in the Privy Purse
accounts of 'lost at the butts to my lord Marquis £1'.
Dorset was the only man in England to hold the
rank of marquis, till his half-sister, Katherine's son,
was created Marquis of Exeter in 1525. He was
chief mourner at the funeral of Katherine's husband
and, towards the end of her life, he visited her in
Devonshire.

The marquis's grandson, named Henry Grey, married Frances Brandon, the daughter of the Duke of
Suffolk, second husband of Mary Tudor, youngest
daughter of Henry VII. Frances Brandon and the
third Marquis of Dorset, who eventually became
Duke of Suffolk, were the parents of Lady Jane
Grey, so that Elizabeth Woodville was the ancestress of every reigning sovereign of England since
Henry VII, even of the nine days' Queen Jane.

Before Elizabeth died, she had one more grief
added to her many griefs, by the knowledge that
every male member of the Woodville family was
dead, and that none of them left any legitmate
children behind to carry on the ancestral name.
Lionel Woodville fled to Brittany at the time of
Buckingham's rebellion, and died abroad before
1484. Sir Edward Woodville was made governor
of the Isle of Wight by Henry VII and he seems
to have been a good soldier though a rash man.
He took it on himself to raise a force of four

hundred men in the Island, and to go to the
assistance of the Duke of Brittany, whose country
was being invaded by France. Perhaps it was as well
for him that he was killed in battle, for he incurred
Henry's anger by this unauthorised procedure, and
probably Sir Edward would have experienced a pro-
longed sojourn in the Tower, even if he had escaped
the axe.

Sir Richard Woodville succeeded his brother
Anthony as third Earl Rivers. He left no children
and when he died he provided in his will 'for a bell
to be tenor at Grafton to the bells there now, for a
remembrance of the last of the blood'.

APPENDICES

APPENDIX I

THE MANOR OF GRAFTON AND
THE WOODVILLE ANCESTRY

Grafton was an ancient manor, called Grastone in Domesday Book, which had been in the occupation of the family for generations. In the time of Henry II it belonged to the Abbey of Grestein, in Normandy, to which it had been given by the grandson of the Earl of Moreton—stepfather of William the Conqueror—who obtained the lands at the Conquest.

The Woodvilles, Widvilles, or Wydevills, had already lived at Grafton since the twelfth century, but only as tenants. In the reign of Henry II, William de Widville held lands there which he left to a line of successors who gradually became richer and more important. In the twenty-fifth year of Edward I, John de Wydeville was returned from the county of Northamptonshire as holding lands, and summoned to perform military service in person, with horse and arms, in parts beyond the seas. His grandson Richard, one of the most influential men in the county, filled the office of high sheriff no less than eight times in the reign of Edward III, and was one of its representatives in seven parliaments. The same county honours were almost as frequently conferred on his son, John Widville, and grandson, Thomas Widville, who became lord of Grafton in the thirteenth year of Henry VI. Thomas was succeeded by his brother Richard, the father of Sir Richard, who married the Duchess of Bedford.

This Richard was Lieutenant of the Tower, and he appears in the third scene of Shakespeare's *King Henry VI,*

Part 1, defending it against Humphrey, Duke of Gloucester, the King's turbulent uncle, who was then engaged in a private brawl with Cardinal Beaufort. The Woodville of this play has only two speeches, and is called 'faint-hearted Woodville' by the angry Duke, but in real life he played a more important role. He was body squire to Henry V and chamberlain to the Duke of Bedford. His son was knighted by Henry VI on that Whit-Sunday in 1426 when the little King, just five years old, was himself knighted by his uncle Bedford, and then afterwards knighted his cousin Richard of York and a band of other youths of good family.

APPENDIX 2

The Letters of Sir Hugh Johns

It was thought for a long time that the two following letters were addressed to Elizabeth Woodville. Transcripts of these letters are in the British Museum, and they were quoted by Miss Strickland and the *Dictionary of National Biography*; but it has now been discovered that they were written to a Dame Elizabeth Wodehille. One is from Richard, Duke of York, the father of Edward IV, and one from the Earl of Warwick, both of whom endeavoured to persuade Dame Wodehille, a wealthy widow, to marry Sir Hugh Johns, a poor knight. Although Dame Wodehille has nothing to do with our story, the letters themselves are of interest as coming from the Duke of York and the Earl of Warwick.

'To Dame Elizabeth Wodehille.

'Right trusty and well-beloved, we greet you well.

'Forasmuch as we are credibly informed that our right hearty and well-beloved knight Sir Hugh Johns for the great womanhood and gentleness approved and known in your person—ye being sole, and to be married—his heart wholly have; wherewith we are right well pleased. Howbeit

APPENDIX 2

your disposition towards him in that behalf, as yet, is to us unknown. We therefore, as for the faithful, true, and good lordship we owe unto him at this time, (and so will continue,) desire and heartily pray ye will on your part be to him well-willed to the performing of this our writing and his desire. Wherein ye shall do not only to our pleasure, but, we doubt not, to your own great weal and worship in time to come; certifying, that if ye fulfil our intent in this matter, we will and shall be to him and you such lord, as shall be to both your great weal and worship, by the grace of God, who precede and guide you in all heavenly felicity and welfare.

'Written by RICHARD, DUKE OF YORK'

'To DAME ELIZABETH WODEHILLE.

'Worshipful and well-beloved, I greet you well: And forasmuch my right well-beloved Sir Hugh Johns knight, (which now late was with you unto his full great joy, and had great cheer, as he said, whereof I thank you,) hath informed me how that he hath, for the great love and affection that he hath unto your person, as well as for the great sadness and wisdom that he hath found and proved in you at that time, as for your great and praised beauty and womanly demeaning, he desireth with all haste to do you worship by way of marriage, before any other creature living, (as he saith). I (considering his said desire, and the great worship that he had, which was made knight at Jerusalem, and after his coming home, for the great wisdom and manhood that he was renowned of, was made knight-marshal of France, and after knight-marshal of England, unto his great worship, with other his great and many virtues and desert, and also the good and notable service that he hath done and daily doth to me,) write unto you at this time, and pray you *effectuously* that ye will the rather (at this my request and prayer) to condescend and apply you unto his said lawful and honest desire, wherein ye shall not only *purvey* right notably for yourself unto your weal and worship in time to come, as I hereby trust, but also cause me to show unto you such good lordship as ye by reason of it shall hold you content and pleased, with the grace of God, which everlastingly have you in his bliss, protection, and governance.

'Written by the EARL OF WARWICK'

APPENDIX 3

THE SUBJECT OF ELIZABETH WOODVILLE'S SUIT TO EDWARD IV

Mr. George Smith in his book, *The Coronation of Elizabeth Wydeville*, has gone very carefully into the subject of Elizabeth's petition to the King, and the following notes are reprinted with his kind permission.

There are amongst the early proceedings in Chancery some pleas which may very well have been the actual

cause of Elizabeth's petition to the King, and their result-
ant love story and marriage.

Sir John Grey's father Edward died in 1457, and by
May, 1462, his mother Elizabeth, now styled Lady
Ferrers, had married again her second husband, being
Sir John Bourchier, one of the sons of Henry Earl of Essex
and his wife Isabella Plantagenet, aunt to Edward IV.

There is a petition to the Lord Chancellor from Sir
John Bourchier and his wife Elizabeth, Lady Ferrers,
asking that the Lord Chancellor would require Robert
Isham, William Boldon, and William Fielding, the
surviving feofees of the manors of Newbotell and Brington
in Northampton and of Woodham Ferrers in the County
of Essex to 'make astate' to her.

There are also two petitions from Dame Elizabeth
Grey to the Lord Chancellor, reciting that by the agreement for her marriage to John Grey made by her father
Richard Wydeville, Lord Rivers, with Sir Edward Grey,
the former on his part undertook to pay a sum of CC
marks, whilst the latter and his wife enfeoffed these three
manors to provide an income for John Grey and his wife
and their heirs. Though Robert Isham and William
Boldon had taken the necessary steps to 'make astate'
to Sir John Grey's widow, William Fielding hesitated to
do so. A further petition from Lord Rivers states that he
had paid his daughter's marriage portion to Sir Edward
Grey, Lord Ferrers, but for the trust that he had in him
took no receipt nor discharge, and now Sir Edward's
widow was dunning him for CXXV marks of the marriage
portion.

In their answers Robert Isham and William Boldon
set out that the intent of the assignment was to provide
an income of one hundred marks yearly 'for the saide
John Grey and Elizabeth his wife, and to the heires of

the said John's bodie'. William Fielding was non-committal in his answer, saying 'that he was uncertain as to the intent of the assignment'.

It is evident that the claims of Lady Elizabeth and her sons to these manors were preferred to those of her mother-in-law, Lady Ferrers. At any rate the matter would seem to have been settled in her favour before she entered into negotiations with William, Lord Hastings, Edward's Chamberlain, for the marriage of one of her sons to his unborn daughter. The matter may have been in course of arrangement for some time, but the agreement (which is recorded in the report of the Hist. MSS. Com. for 1928) was signed by her under the date 13th April, 1464. It is an indenture 'made between Elizabeth Grey, widow of Sir John Grey, knight, son and heir of Edward Grey, late Lord Ferrers, and William, Lord Hastings for the marriage of Thomas Grey, her son or in case of his death of Richard his brother, with the eldest daughter to be born within the next five or six years to Lord Hastings; or failing such a daughter with one of the daughters to be born within the same period to Ralph Hastings, his brother, or, failing such a daughter with one of the daughters of Dame Anne Ferrers his sister. If any manors or possessions once belonging to Sir William Asteley, knight, called "Asteley lands" or any of the inheritance of dame Elizabeth "called Lady Ferrers of Groby" (save all manors, lands, and tenements in Nobottle (Newbotell) and Brington, co. North hants. and Woodham Ferrers, co. Essex) were at any time recovered in the title and right of Thomas or Richard from the possession of any other person having an interest in them, half of the rent and profits thereof while Thomas or, if he died, Richard, was under age of twelve years was to belong to Lord Hastings and half to dame Elizabeth. Lord Hastings to pay her the sum of 500 marks for the marriage, but if both Thomas or Richard died before such marriage, or if there was no female issue as above she to pay him the sum of 250 marks'.

Although this agreement was not fulfilled, it is not uninteresting that Elizabeth's son Thomas eventually married, not Lord Hastings's daughter, but his step-daughter, Cecily, the daughter of Lady Hastings, by her first husband, William Bonville, Lord Harington.

The heir to the Asteley lands had been Sir Edward Grey, Sir John's father.

It was all too clear to Elizabeth that in the circumstances of her mother-in-law's marriage, these lands as well as the property which Lady Ferrers herself had inherited, might pass away to the Bourchiers, unless some-one sufficiently strong was able to uphold her children's claims. So it would seem that in the interests of her children, she had entered into this agreement with Hastings, who was on terms of intimate friendship with the King, and able to wield an influence which even that of the Bourchier family could not easily override.

In the same month a belated inquiry was made into the affairs of her late husband Sir John Grey establishing that their son Thomas was heir.

By the agreement with Lord Hastings and the official recognition of her eldest son as heir to his father Sir John Grey, Elizabeth probably felt that her children's interests were safeguarded as far as possible.

APPENDIX 4

Fifteenth Century Banquets

There is no record of the actual dishes served at the coronation banquet of Elizabeth Woodville, but from the descriptions of other fifteenth century feasts it is possible to form an idea of what was eaten.

The banquet was divided into three courses, and each course was a complete meal consisting of fish, meat, and sweets. Anything upwards of twenty dishes composed a course, and each course was carried into the hall in a procession which, at the coronation banquet, was preceded by a man on horseback. The crowning glory of the course was the 'Sotyltye' which was carried in at the end of the procession, and which was a triumph of the confectioner's art. It was composed of sugar, paste, and other plastic ingredients, and was coloured and gilded, and adorned with mottoes. It was highly allegorical and probably supplied a fruitful subject of conversation during the meal, and a certain source of indigestion afterwards.

These subtleties of course always bore on the occasion for which they were devised, and when in 1443 John Stafford was installed as Archbishop of Canterbury, the confectioner had to devise something with an ecclesiastical flavour. It was 'Saint Andrew sitting on an high altar of estate, with beams of gold: afore him kneeling the bishop in pontificalibus; his crozier kneeling behind him coped'.

At the coronation banquet of Henry VI in 1429, there were three courses and three 'sotyltyes'; one represented the King with St Edward and St Louis; another the King kneeling between his father, Henry V, and the Emperor Sigismund; and the third 'our Lady sitting with her child in her lap, and she holding a crown in her hand. Saint George and Saint Denis, kneeling on either side, presented to her King Henry's figure, bearing in his hand a ballad'.

The dishes which were less ornamental but more eatable included jelly[1] 'written and noted with Te Deum

---

[1] Aspic jelly.

Laudamus', boar's head, cygnet, heron, pike, crane, bittern, partridge, peacock, bream, quinces in compost, venison, egrets, curlew, plover, quails, snipe, 'great birds,' larks, carp and crab, besides such pretty sweets as 'Custard royal, with a leopard of gold sitting therein and holding a fleur de lys', and 'a fritter garnished with a leopard's head and two ostrich feathers'.

The coronation banquet of Katharine of France, on 23rd February, 1421, appears, by the astonishing variety of fish which was served, to have fallen in Lent. Although the first course starts with brawn with mustard, it goes on to pike, lamprey, powdered great eels, trout, codling, plaice, and merlin fried and 'crabs great'. Then came a made dish 'flourished with collars of SS and broom-pods' (a compliment to the Plantagenet family) and a shield with the arms of 'the King and Queen departed' presumably the parents of Henry V. After this came "a Sublety called a pelican on her nest, with birds, and an image of Saint Katharine, with a wheel in her hand, disputing with the Heathen clerks, having this Reason (motto) in her hand. Madame la Roigne: the Pelican answering Cest enseigne: the birds answering Est du roy pur tenir joie. A tout gent il met sentant'.

The second course was quite as long. It began with 'jelly flourished with columbine flowers', blaundesore (blancdesire, a compound mess, usually made of chicken pounded with milk of almonds, rice flour, wheat starch, sugar, and lard, and then moulded and 'served forth'); then followed bream, conger, soles with mullet, barbel with roach, salmon fresh, lobsters, lampreys, and a made dish 'written with the kings words: Une sans plus', in white letters. Then the subtlety: a panther, with an image of St Katharine holding a wheel in one hand, and a Reason in the other.

APPENDIX 5

The third course began with 'dates in compost' and 'creme motley'; it continued with carp, dory, turbot, tench, perch, sturgeon, whelks, porpoise, crawfish (creves de ewe douce) prawns (shrympes grosse), two made dishes, one in the form of a Katharine wheel, an allusion which must by now have become plain to the meanest intelligence, and the other ornamented with green hawthorn leaves and red haws. Then a remarkable subtlety of 'a tiger looking in a mirror and a man riding on horseback carrying a tiger whelp in his barme and throwing mirrors for his defence'.

APPENDIX 5

LETTER OF ELIZABETH WOODVILLE TO SIR WILLIAM STONER[1]

By the Queen.

Trusty and well-beloved, we greet you well, And whereas we understand, by report, made unto us at this time, that you have taken upon you now of late to make masteries within our forest and chace of Barnwood and Excill, and there, in contempt of us, uncourteously to hunt and slay our deer within the same, to our great marvel and displeasure; we will you wit that we intend to sue such remedy therein as shall accord with my lord's laws. And whereas we farthermore understand that you purpose, under colour of my lord's commission, in that behalf granted unto you as you say, hastily to take the view and rule of our game of deer within our said forest and chase; we will that you shew unto us or our council your said commission, if any such you have, and, in the mean season, that you spare of hunting within our said

[1] Sir William Stoner filled the office of Constable of Wallingford Castle and other royal demesnes.

243

forest or chace, as you will answer at your peril. Given under our signet, at our manor of Greenwich, the first day of August.

ELIZABETH

To our trusty and well-beloved Sir
William Stoner, Knight

APPENDIX 6

The following passages from Shakespeare have reference to scenes which are described in this book :—

III HENRY VI. ACT III

SCENE II. LONDON. THE PALACE

Enter KING EDWARD, GLOUCESTER, CLARENCE, *and* LADY
GREY.

K. EDW. Brother of Gloucester, at Saint Alban's field
  This lady's husband, Sir Richard Grey, was slain,
  His lands then seized on by the conqueror:
  Her suit is now to repossess those lands;
  Which we in justice cannot well deny,
  Because in quarrel of the house of York
  The worthy gentleman did lose his life.
GLOU. Your highness shall do well to grant her suit;
  It were dishonour to deny it her.
K. EDW. It were no less; but yet I'll make a pause.
GLOU. [*aside to* CLAR.] Yea, is it so?
  I see the lady hath a thing to grant,
  Before the king will grant her humble suit.
CLAR. [*aside to* GLOU.] He knows the game: how true he
    keeps the wind!
GLOU. [*aside to* CLAR.] Silence!

K. EDW. Widow, we will consider of your suit;
And come some other time to know our mind.

L. GREY. Right gracious lord, I cannot brook delay:
May it please your highness to resolve me now;
And what your pleasure is, shall satisfy me.

GLOU. [*aside to* CLAR.] Ay, widow? then I'll warrant you
all your lands,
An if what pleases him shall pleasure you.
Fight closer, or, good faith, you'll catch a blow.

CLAR. [*aside to* GLOU.] I fear her not, unless she chance
to fall.

GLOU. [*aside to* CLAR.] God forbid that! for he'll take
vantages.

K. EDW. How many children hast thou, widow? tell me.

CLAR. [*aside to* GLOU.] I think he means to beg a child
of her.

GLOU. [*aside to* CLAR.] Nay, whip me then: he'll rather
give her two.

L. GREY. Three, my most gracious lord.

GLOU. [*aside to* CLAR.] You shall have four, if you'll be
ruled by him.

K. EDW. 'Twere pity they should lose their father's lands.

L. GREY. Be pitiful, dread lord, and grant it then.

K. EDW. Lords, give us leave: I'll try this widow's wit.

GLOU. [*aside to* CLAR.] Ay, good leave have you; for you
will have leave,
Till youth take leave and leave you to the crutch.
[GLOUCESTER *and* CLARENCE *retire.*

K. EDW. Now tell me, madam, do you love your
children?

L. GREY. Ay, full as dearly as I love myself.

K. EDW. And would you not do much to do them good?

L. GREY. To do them good, I would sustain some harm.

K. EDW. Then get your husband's lands, to do them good.

L. Grey. Therefore I came unto your majesty.

K. Edw. I'll tell you how these lands are to be got.

L. Grey. So shall you bind me to your highness' service.

K. Edw. What service wilt thou do me, if I give them?

L. Grey. What you command, that rests in me to do.

K. Edw. But you will take exceptions to my boon.

L. Grey. No, gracious lord, except I cannot do it.

K. Edw. Ay, but thou canst do what I mean to ask.

L. Grey. Why, then I will do what your grace commands.

Glou. [*aside to* Clar.] He plies her hard; and much rain wears the marble.

Clar. [*aside to* Glou.] As red as fire! nay, then her wax must melt.

L. Grey. Why stops my lord? shall I not hear my task?

K. Edw. An easy task; 'tis but to love a king.

L. Grey. That's soon perform'd, because I am a subject.

K. Edw. Why, then, thy husband's lands I freely give thee.

L. Grey. I take my leave with many thousand thanks.

Glou. [*aside to* Clar.] The match is made; she seals it with a curtsy.

K. Edw. But stay thee, 'tis the fruits of love I mean.

L. Grey. The fruits of love I mean, my loving liege.

K. Edw. Ay, but, I fear me, in another sense.
What love, think'st thou, I sue so much to get?

L. Grey. My love till death, my humble thanks, my prayers;
That love which virtue begs and virtue grants.

K. Edw. No, by my troth, I did not mean such love.

L. Grey. Why, then you mean not as I thought you did.

K. Edw. But now you partly may perceive my mind.

L. Grey. My mind will never grant what I perceive
Your highness aims at, if I aim aright.

246

K. Edw. To tell thee plain, I aim to lie with thee.

L. Grey. To tell you plain, I had rather lie in prison.

K. Edw. Why, then thou shalt not have thy husband's
lands.

L. Grey. Why, then mine honesty shall be my dower;
For by that loss I will not purchase them.

K. Edw. Therein thou wrong'st thy children mightily.

L. Grey. Herein your highness wrongs both them and me.
But, mighty lord, this merry inclination
Accords not with the sadness of my suit:
Please you dismiss me, either with 'ay' or 'no'.

K. Edw. Ay, if thou wilt say 'ay' to my request;
No, if thou dost say 'no' to my demand.

L. Grey. Then, no, my lord. My suit is at an end.

Glou. [aside to Clar.] The widow likes him not, she knits
her brows.

Clar. [aside to Glou.] He is the bluntest wooer in
Christendom.

K. Edw. [aside.] Her looks do argue her replete with
modesty;
Her words do show her wit incomparable;
All her perfections challenge sovereignty:
One way or other, she is for a king;
And she shall be my love, or else my queen.—
Say that King Edward take thee for his queen?

L. Grey. 'Tis better said than done, my gracious lord:
I am a subject fit to jest withal,
But far unfit to be a sovereign.

K. Edw. Sweet widow, by my state I swear to thee
I speak no more than what my soul intends;
And that is, to enjoy thee for my love.

L. Grey. And that is more than I will yield unto:
I know I am too mean to be your queen,
And yet too good to be your concubine.

K. EDW. You cavil, widow: I did mean, my queen.

L. GREY. 'Twill grieve your grace my sons should call
   you father.

K. EDW. No more than when my daughters call thee
   mother.
   Thou art a widow, and thou hast some children;
   And, by God's mother, I, being but a bachelor,
   Have other some: why, 'tis a happy thing
   To be the father unto many sons.
   Answer no more, for thou shalt be my queen.

GLOU. [*aside to* CLAR.] The ghostly father now hath done
   his shrift.

CLAR. [*aside to* GLOU.] When he was made a shriver, 'twas
   for shift.

K. EDW. Brothers you muse what chat we two have had.

GLOU. The widow likes it not, for she looks very sad.

K. EDW. You'ld think it strange if I should marry her.

CLAR. To whom, my lord?

K. EDW.   Why, Clarence, to myself.

GLOU. That would be ten days' wonder at the least.

CLAR. That's a day longer than a wonder lasts.

GLOU. By so much is the wonder in extremes.

K. EDW. Well, jest on, brothers: I can tell you both
   Her suit is granted for her husband's lands.

ACT IV

SCENE I. LONDON. THE PALACE

Enter GLOUCESTER, CLARENCE, SOMERSET, *and* MONTAGUE.

GLOU. Now tell me, brother Clarence, what think you
   Of this new marriage with the Lady Grey?
   Hath not our brother made a worthy choice?

CLAR. Alas, you know, 'tis far from hence to France;
   How could he stay till Warwick made return?

Som. My lords, forbear this talk; here comes the king.
Glou. And his well-chosen bride.
Clar. I mind to tell him plainly what I think.

Flourish. Enter KING EDWARD, *attended;* LADY GREY,
as Queen; PEMBROKE, STAFFORD, HASTINGS, *and others.*

K. EDW. Now, brother of Clarence, how like you our
  choice,
That you stand pensive, as half malcontent?
CLAR. As well as Lewis of France, or the Earl of Warwick,
Which are so weak of courage and in judgement
That they'll take no offence at our abuse.
K. EDW. Suppose they take offence without a cause,
They are but Lewis and Warwick: I am Edward,
Your king and Warwick's, and must have my will.
GLOU. And shall have your will, because our king:
Yet hasty marriage seldom proveth well.
K. EDW. Yea, brother Richard, are you offended too?
GLOU. Not I:
No, God forbid that I should wish them sever'd
Whom God hath join'd together; ay, and 'twere pity
To sunder them that yoke so well together.
K. EDW. Setting your scorns and your mislike aside,
Tell me some reason why the Lady Grey
Should not become my wife and England's queen.
And you too, Somerset and Montague,
Speak freely what you think.
CLAR. Then this is mine opinion: that King Lewis
Becomes your enemy, for mocking him
About the marriage of the Lady Bona.
GLOU. And Warwick, doing what you gave in charge,
Is now dishonoured by this new marriage.
K. EDW. What if both Lewis and Warwick be appeased
By such invention as I can devise?

MONT. Yet, to have join'd with France in such alliance
Would more have strengthen'd this our commonwealth
'Gainst foreign storms than any home-bred marriage.

HAST. Why, knows not Montague that of itself
England is safe, if true within itself?

MONT. But the safer when 'tis back'd with France.

HAST. 'Tis better using France than trusting France:
Let us be back'd with God, and with the seas
Which He hath given for fence impregnable,
And with their helps only defend ourselves;
In them and in ourselves our safety lies.

CLAR. For this one speech Lord Hastings well deserves
To have the heir of the Lord Hungerford.

K. EDW. Ay, what of that? it was my will and grant;
And for this once my will shall stand for law.

GLOU. And yet methinks your grace hath not done well,
To give the heir and daughter of Lord Scales
Unto the brother of your loving bride;
She better would have fitted me or Clarence:
But in your bride you bury brotherhood.

CLAR. Or else you would not have bestow'd the heir
Of the Lord Bonville on your new wife's son,
And leave your brothers to go speed elsewhere.

K. EDW. Alas, poor Clarence! is it for a wife
That thou art malcontent? I will provide thee.

CLAR. In choosing for yourself, you show'd your judgement,
Which being shallow, you shall give me leave
To play the broker in mine own behalf;
And to that end I shortly mind to leave you.

K. EDW. Leave me, or tarry, Edward will be king,
And not be tied unto his brother's will.

Q. ELIZ. My lords, before it pleased his majesty
To raise my state to title of a queen,

Do me but right, and you must all confess
That I was not ignoble of descent;
And meaner than myself have had like fortune.
But as this title honours me and mine,
So your dislike, to whom I would be pleasing,
Doth cloud my joys with danger and with sorrow.

K. Edw. My love, forbear to fawn upon their frowns:
What danger or what sorrow can befall thee.
So long as Edward is thy constant friend,
And their true sovereign, whom they must obey?
Nay, whom they shall obey, and love thee too,
Unless they seek for hatred at my hands;
Which if they do, yet will I keep thee safe,
And they shall feel the vengeance of my wrath.

Glou. [*aside.*] I hear, yet say not much, but think the
more.

ACT IV

Scene IV. London. The Palace

Enter Queen Elizabeth *and* Rivers.

Riv. Madam, what makes you in this sudden change?

Q. Eliz. Why, brother Rivers, are you yet to learn
What late misfortune is befall'n King Edward?

Riv. What! loss of some pitch'd battle against Warwick?

Q. Eliz. No, but the loss of his own royal person.

Riv. Then is my sovereign slain?

Q. Eliz. Ay, almost slain, for he is taken prisoner,
Either betray'd by falsehood of his guard
Or by his foe surprised at unawares:
And, as I further have to understand,
Is new committed to the Bishop of York,
Fell Warwick's brother and by that our foe.

251

RIV.   These news I must confess are full of grief;
  Yet, gracious madam, bear it as you may:
  Warwick may lose, that now hath won the day.
Q. ELIZ.   Till then fair hope must hinder life's decay.
  And I the rather wean me from despair
  For love of Edward's offspring in my womb:
  This is it that makes me bridle passion
  And bear with mildness my misfortune's cross;
  Ay, ay, for this I draw in many a tear
  And stop the rising of blood-sucking sighs,
  Lest with my sighs or tears I blast or drown
  King Edward's fruit, true heir to the English crown.
RIV.   But, madam, where is Warwick then become?
Q. ELIZ.   I am inform'd that he comes towards London,
  To set the crown once more on Henry's head:
  Guess thou the rest: King Edward's friends must down,
  But, to prevent the tyrant's violence,—
  For trust not him that hath once broken faith,—
  I'll hence forthwith unto the sanctuary,
  To save at least the heir of Edward's right:
  There shall I rest secure from force and fraud.
  Come, therefore, let us fly while we may fly:
  If Warwick take us we are sure to die.   [exeunt.

ACT V

SCENE VII. LONDON. THE PALACE

Flourish.   Enter KING EDWARD, QUEEN ELIZABETH,
  CLARENCE, GLOUCESTER, HASTINGS, *a* NURSE *with the
  young Prince, and* ATTENDANTS.

K. EDW.   Once more we sit in England's royal throne,
  Re-purchased with the blood of enemies.
  What valiant foemen, like to autumn's corn,
  Have we mow'd down in tops of all their pride!

Three Dukes of Somerset, threefold renown'd
For hardy and undoubted champions;
Two Cliffords, as the father and the son,
And two Northumberlands; two braver men
Ne'er spurr'd their coursers at the trumpet's sound;
With them, the two brave bears, Warwick and
   Montague,
That in their chains fetter'd the kingly lion
And made the forest tremble when they roar'd.
Thus have we swept suspicion from our seat
And made our footstool of security.
Come hither, Bess, and let me kiss my boy.
Young Ned, for thee, thine uncles and myself
Have in our armours watch'd the winter's night,
Went all afoot in summer's scalding heat,
That thou mightst repossess the crown in peace;
And of our labours thou shalt reap the gain.
GLOU. [*aside.*] I'll blast his harvest, if your head were laid;
For yet I am not look'd on in the world.
This shoulder was ordain'd so thick to heave;
And heave it shall some weight, or break my back:
Work thou the way,—and thou shalt execute.
K. EDW. Clarence and Gloucester, love my lovely
   queen;
And kiss your princely nephew, brothers both.
CLAR. The duty that I owe unto your majesty
I seal upon the lips of this sweet babe.
Q. ELIZ. Thanks, noble Clarence; worthy brother,
   thanks.
GLOU. And, that I love the tree from whence thou
   sprang'st,
Witness the loving kiss I give the fruit.
[*aside.*] To say the truth, so Judas kiss'd his master,
And cried 'all hail!' when as he meant all harm.

THE FIRST QUEEN ELIZABETH

K. EDW. Now am I seated as my soul delights,
Having my country's peace and brother's loves.
CLAR. What will your grace have done with Margaret?
Reignier, her father, to the king of France
Hath pawn'd the Sicils and Jerusalem,
And hither have they sent it for her ransom.
K. EDW. Away with her, and waft her hence to France.
And now what rests but that we spend the time
With stately triumphs, mirthful comic shows,
Such as befits the pleasure of the court?
Sound drums and trumpets! farewell sour annoy!
For here, I hope, begins our lasting joy.   [exeunt.

RICHARD III. ACT I
SCENE III. THE PALACE

Enter QUEEN ELIZABETH, LORD RIVERS, *and* LORD GREY.

RIV. Have patience, madam: there's no doubt his majesty
Will soon recover his accustom'd health.
GREY. In that you brook it ill, it makes him worse:
Therefore, for God's sake, entertain good comfort,
And cheer his grace with quick and merry words.
Q. ELIZ. If he were dead, what would betide of me?
RIV. No other harm but loss of such a lord.
Q. ELIZ. The loss of such a lord includes all harm.
GREY. The heavens have bless'd you with a goodly son,
To be your comforter when he is gone.
Q. ELIZ. Oh, he is young, and his minority
Is put unto the trust of Richard Gloucester,
A man that loves not me, nor none of you.
RIV. Is it concluded he shall be protector?
Q. ELIZ. It is determined, not concluded yet:
But so it must be, if the king miscarry.

Enter BUCKINGHAM *and* DERBY.

254

GREY. Here come the lords of Buckingham and Derby.

BUCK. Good time of day unto your royal grace!

DER. God make your majesty joyful as you have been!

Q. ELIZ. The Countess Richmond, good my lord of
Derby,
To your good prayers will scarcely say amen.
Yet, Derby, notwithstanding she's your wife,
And loves not me, be you, good lord, assured
I hate not you for her proud arrogance.

DER. I do beseech you, either not believe
The envious slanders of her false accusers;
Or, if she be accused in true report,
Bear with her weakness, which, I think, proceeds
From wayward sickness, and no grounded malice.

RIV. Saw you the king to-day, my Lord of Derby?

DER. But now the Duke of Buckingham and I
Are come from visiting his majesty.

Q. ELIZ. What likelihood of his amendment, lords?

BUCK. Madam, good hope; his grace speaks cheerfully.

Q. ELIZ. God grant him health! Did you confer with
him?

BUCK. Madam, we did: he desires to make atonement
Betwixt the Duke of Gloucester and your brothers,
And betwixt them and my lord chamberlain;
And sent to warn them to his royal presence.

Q. ELIZ. Would all were well! but that will never be:
I fear our happiness is at the highest.

Enter GLOUCESTER, HASTINGS, *and* DORSET.

GLOU. They do me wrong, and I will not endure it:
Who are they that complain unto the king,
That I, forsooth, am stern and love them not?
By holy Paul, they love his grace but lightly
That fill his ears with such dissentious rumours.

Because I cannot flatter and speak fair,
Smile in men's faces, smooth, deceive and cog,
Duck with French nods and apish courtesy,
I must be held a rancorous enemy.
Cannot a plain man live and think no harm,
But thus his simple truth must be abused
By silken, sly, insinuating Jacks?

RIV. To whom in all this presence speaks you grace.

GLOU. To thee, that hast nor honesty nor grace.
When have I injured thee? when done thee wrong?
Or thee? or thee? or any of your faction?
A plague upon you all! His royal person,—
Whom God preserve better than you would wish!—
Cannot be quiet scarce a breathing-while,
But you must trouble him with lewd complaints.

Q. ELIZ. Brother of Gloucester, you mistake the matter.
The king, of his own royal disposition,
And not provoked by any suitor else;
Aiming, belike, at your interior hatred,
Which in your outward actions shows itself
Against my kindred, brothers, and myself,
Makes him to send; that thereby he may gather
The ground of your ill-will, and so remove it.

GLOU. I cannot tell: the world is grown so bad,
That wrens make prey where eagles dare not perch:
Since every Jack became a gentleman,
There's many a gentle person made a Jack.

Q. ELIZ. Come, come, we know your meaning, brother
Gloucester;
You envy my advancement and my friends':
God grant we never may have need of you!

GLOU. Meantime, God grants that we have need of you:
Our brother is imprison'd by your means,
Myself disgraced, and the nobility

256

Held in contempt; whilst many fair promotions
Are daily given to ennoble those
That scarce, some two days since, were worth a
    noble.

Q. ELIZ. By Him that raised me to this careful height
From that contented hap which I enjoy'd,
I never did incense his majesty
Against the Duke of Clarence, but have been
An earnest advocate to plead for him.
My lord, you do me shameful injury,
Falsely to draw me in these vile suspects.

GLOU. You may deny that you were not the cause
Of my Lord Hastings' late imprisonment.

RIV. She may, my lord, for—

GLOU. She may, Lord Rivers! why, who knows not so?
She may do more, sir, than denying that:
She may help you to many fair preferments;
And then deny her aiding hand therein,
And lay those honours on your high deserts.
What may she not? She may, yea, marry, may she,—

RIV. What, marry, may she?

GLOU. What, marry, may she! marry with a king,
A bachelor, a handsome stripling too:
I wis your grandam had a worser match.

Q. ELIZ. My Lord of Gloucester, I have too long borne
Your blunt upbraidings and your bitter scoffs:
By heaven, I will acquaint his majesty
With those gross taunts I often have endured.
I had rather be a country servant-maid
Than a great queen, with this condition,
To be thus taunted, scorn'd, and baited at:

Enter QUEEN MARGARET, *behind.*

Small joy have I in being England's queen.

THE FIRST QUEEN ELIZABETH

Q. MAR. And lessen'd be that small, God, I beseech thee!
  Thy honour, state and seat is due to me.
GLOU. What! threat you me with telling of the king?
  Tell him, and spare not: look, what I have said
  I will avouch in presence of the king:
  I dare adventure to be sent to the Tower.
  'Tis time to speak; my pains are quite forgot.
Q. MAR. Out, devil! I remember them too well:
  Thou slewest my husband Henry in the Tower,
  And Edward, my poor son, at Tewksbury.
GLOU. Ere you were queen, yea, or your husband king,
  I was a pack-horse in his great affairs;
  A weeder-out of his proud adversaries,
  A liberal rewarder of his friends:
  To royalise his blood I spilt mine own.
Q. MAR. Yea, and much better blood than his or thine.
GLOU. In all which time you and your husband Grey
  Were factious for the house of Lancaster;
  And, Rivers, so were you. Was not your husband
  In Margaret's battle at Saint Alban's slain?
  Let me put in your minds, if you forget,
  What you have been ere now, and what you are;
  Withal, what I have been, and what I am.
Q. MAR. A murderous villain, and so still thou art.
GLOU. Poor Clarence did forsake his father, Warwick;
  Yea, and foreswore himself,—which Jesu pardon!—
Q. MAR. Which God revenge!
GLOU. To fight on Edward's party for the crown;
  And for his meed, poor lord, he is mew'd up.
  I would to God my heart were flint, like Edward's;
  Or Edward's soft and pitiful, like mine:
  I am too childish-foolish for this world.
Q. MAR. Hie thee to hell for shame, and leave the world,
  Thou cacodemon! there thy kingdom is.

RIV. My Lord of Gloucester, in those busy days
  Which here you urge to prove us enemies,
  We follow'd then our lord, our lawful king:
  So should we you, if you should be our king.
GLOU. If I should be! I had rather be a pedlar:
  Far be if from my heart, the thought of it!
Q. ELIZ. As little joy, my lord, as you suppose
  You should enjoy, were you this country's king,
  As little joy may you suppose in me,
  That I enjoy, being the queen thereof.
Q. MAR. A little joy enjoys the queen thereof;
  For I am she, and altogether joyless.
  I can no longer hold me patient.   [advancing.
  Hear me, you wrangling pirates, that fall out
  In sharing that which you have pill'd from me!
  Which of you trembles not that looks on me?
  If not, that, I being queen, you bow like subjects,
  Yet that, by you deposed, you quake like rebels?
  O gentle villain, do not turn away!
GLOU. Foul wrinkled witch, what makest thou in my
    sight?
Q. MAR. But repetition of what thou hast marr'd;
  That will I make before I let thee go.
GLOU. Wert thou not banished on pain of death?
Q. MAR. I was; but I do find more pain in banishment
  Than death can yield me here by my abode.
  A husband and a son thou owest to me;
  And thou a kingdom; all of you allegiance:
  The sorrow that I have, by right is yours,
  And all the pleasures you usurp are mine.
GLOU. The curse my noble father laid on thee,
  When thou didst crown his warlike brows with paper
  And with thy scorns drew'st rivers from his eyes,
  And then, to dry them, gavest the duke a clout

Steep'd in the faultless blood of pretty Rutland,—
His curses, then from bitterness of soul
Denounced against thee, are all fall'n upon thee;
And God, not we, hath plagued thy bloody deed.

Q. ELIZ.   So just is God, to right the innocent.

HAST.   O, 'twas the foulest deed to slay that babe,
And the most merciless that e'er was heard of!

RIV.   Tyrants themselves wept when it was reported.

DOR.   No man but prophesied revenge for it.

BUCK.   Northumberland, then present, wept to see it.

Q. MAR.   What! were you snarling all before I came,
Ready to catch each other by the throat,
And turn you all your hatred now on me?
Did York's dread curse prevail so much with heaven
That Henry's death, my lovely Edward's death,
Their kingdom's loss, my woful banishment,
Could all but answer for that peevish brat?
Can curses pierce the clouds and enter heaven?
Why, then, give way, dull clouds, to my quick curses!
If not by war, by surfeit die your king,
As ours by murder, to make him a king!
Edward thy son, which now is Prince of Wales,
For Edward my son, which was Prince of Wales,
Die in his youth by like untimely violence!
Thyself a queen, for me that was a queen,
Outlive thy glory, like my wretched self!
Long mayst thou live to wail thy children's loss;
And see another, as I see thee now,
Deck'd in thy rights, as thou art stall'd in mine!
Long die thy happy days before thy death;
And, after many lengthen'd hours of grief,
Die neither mother, wife, nor England's queen!
Rivers and Dorset, you were standers by,
And so wast thou, Lord Hastings, when my son

KING RICHARD III

Was stabb'd with bloody daggers: God, I pray him,
That none of you may live your natural age,
But by some unlook'd accident cut off!

GLOU. Have done thy charm, thou hateful wither'd hag!

Q. MAR. And leave out thee? stay, dog, for thou shalt
    hear me.
If heaven have any grievous plague in store
Exceeding those that I can wish upon thee,
O, let them keep it till thy sins be ripe,
And then hurl down their indignation
On thee, the troubler of the poor world's peace!
The worm of conscience still begnaw thy soul!
Thy friends suspect for traitors while thou livest,
And take deep traitors for thy dearest friends!
No sleep close up that deadly eye of thine,
Unless it be whilst some tormenting dream
Affrights thee with a hell of ugly devils!
Thou elvish-mark'd, abortive, rooting hog!
Thou that wast seal'd in thy nativity
The slave of nature and the son of hell!
Thou slander of thy mother's heavy womb!
Thou loathed issue of thy father's loins!
Thou rag of honour! thou detested—

GLOU. Margaret.

Q. MAR.   Richard!

GLOU.   Ha!

Q. MAR.   I call thee not.

GLOU. I cry thee mercy then, for I had thought
    That thou hadst call'd me all these bitter names.

Q. MAR. Why, so I did; but look'd for no reply.
    O, let me make the period to my curse!

GLOU. 'Tis done by me, and ends in 'Margaret'.

Q. ELIZ. Thus have you breathed your curse against
    yourself.

Q. MAR. Poor painted queen, vain flourish of my for-
    tune!
Why strew'st thou sugar on that bottled spider,
Whose deadly web ensnareth thee about?
Fool, fool! thou whet'st a knife to kill thyself.
The time will come when thou shalt wish for me
To help thee curse that poisonous bunch-back'd toad.
HAST. False-boding woman, end thy frantic curse,
    Lest to thy harm thou move our patience.
Q. MAR. Foul shame upon you! you have all moved mine.
RIV. Were you well served, you would be taught your
    duty.
Q. MAR. To serve me well, you all should do me duty,
Teach me to be your queen, and you my subjects:
O, serve me well, and teach yourselves that duty!
DOR. Dispute not with her; she is lunatic.
Q. MAR. Peace, master marquess, you are malapert:
Your fire-new stamp of honour is scarce current.
O, that your young nobility could judge
What 'twere to lose it, and be miserable!
They that stand high have many blasts to shake them;
And if they fall, they dash themselves to pieces.
GLOU. Good counsel, marry; learn it, learn it, marquess.
DOR. It toucheth you, my lord, as much as me.
GLOU. Yea, and much more; but I was born so high,
Our aery buildeth in the cedar's top,
And dallies with the wind and scorns the sun.
Q. MAR. And turns the sun to shade; alas! alas!
Witness my son, now in the shade of death;
Whose bright out-shining beams thy cloudy wrath
Hath in eternal darkness folded up.
Your aery buildeth in our aery's nest.
O God, that seest it, do not suffer it;
As it was won with blood, lost be it so!

Buck. Have done! for shame, if not for charity.

Q. Mar. Urge neither charity nor shame to me:
Uncharitably with me have you dealt,
And shamefully by you my hopes are butcher'd.
My charity is outrage, life my shame;
And in that shame still live my sorrow's rage!

Buck. Have done, have done.

Q.Mar. O princely Buckingham, I'll kiss thy hand,
In sign of league and amity with thee:
Now fair befal thee and thy noble house!
Thy garments are not spotted with our blood,
Nor thou within the compass of my curse.

Buck. Nor no one here; for curses never pass
The lips of those that breathe them in the air.

Q. Mar. I'll not believe but they ascend the sky,
And there awake God's gentle-sleeping peace.
O Buckingham, take heed of yonder dog!
Look, when he fawns, he bites; and when he bites,
His venom tooth will rankle to the death:
Have not to do with him, beware of him;
Sin, death, and hell have set their marks on him,
And all their ministers attend on him.

Glou. What doth she say, my Lord of Buckingham?

Buck. Nothing that I respect, my gracious lord.

Q. Mar. What, dost thou scorn me for my gentle
counsel?
And soothe the devil that I warn thee from?
O, but remember this another day,
When he shall split thy very heart with sorrow,
And say poor Margaret was a prophetess!
Live each of you the subjects to his hate,
And he to yours, and all of you to God's!   [exit.

Hast. My hair doth stand on end to hear her curses.

Riv. And so doth mine: I muse why she's at liberty.

THE FIRST QUEEN ELIZABETH

GLOU. I cannot blame her: by God's holy mother,
　　She hath had too much wrong; and I repent
　　My part thereof that I have done to her.
Q. ELIZ. I never did her any, to my knowledge.
GLOU. But you have all the vantage of her wrong.
　　I was too hot to do somebody good,
　　That is too cold in thinking of it now.
　　Marry, as for Clarence, he is well repaid;
　　He is frank'd up to fatting for his pains:
　　God pardon them that are the cause of it!
RIV. A virtuous and a Christian-like conclusion,
　　To pray for them that have done scathe to us.
GLOU. So do I ever: [aside] being well advised.
　　For had I cursed now, I had cursed myself.

Enter CATESBY

CATES. Madam, his majesty doth call for you;
　　And for your grace; and you, my noble lords.
Q. ELIZ. Catesby, we come. Lords, will you go with us?
RIV. Madam, we will attend your grace.
　　　　　　　　　　　[Exeunt all but GLOUCESTER.

ACT II

SCENE I. LONDON. THE PALACE

Flourish. Enter KING EDWARD *sick,* QUEEN ELIZABETH,
　DORSET, RIVERS, HASTINGS, BUCKINGHAM, GREY, *and
　others.*

K. EDW. Why, so: now have I done a good day's work:
　　You peers, continue this united league:
　　I every day expect an embassage
　　From my Redeemer to redeem me hence;
　　And now in peace my soul shall part to heaven,

264

Since I have set my friends at peace on earth.
Rivers and Hastings, take each other's hand;
Dissemble not your hatred, swear your love.

RIV. By heaven, my heart is purged from grudging hate;
And with my hand I seal my true heart's love.

HAST. So thrive I, as I truly swear the like!

K. EDW. Take heed you dally not before your king;
Lest he that is the supreme King of kings
Confound your hidden falsehood, and award
Either of you to be the other's end.

HAST. So prosper I, as I swear perfect love!

RIV. And I, as I love Hastings with my heart!

K. EDW. Madam, yourself are not exempt in this,
Nor your son Dorset, Buckingham, nor you;
You have been factious one against the other.
Wife, love Lord Hastings, let him kiss your hand;
And what you do, do it unfeignedly.

Q. ELIZ. Here, Hastings; I will never more remember
Our former hatred, so thrive I and mine!

K. EDW. Dorset, embrace him; Hastings, love lord
marquess.

DOR. This interchange of love, I here protest,
Upon my part shall be unviolable.

HAST. And so swear I, my lord.   [*They embrace.*

K. EDW. Now, princely Buckingham, seal thou this league
With thy embracements to my wife's allies,
And make me happy in your unity.

BUCK. Whenever Buckingham doth turn his hate
On you or yours [*to the* QUEEN], but with all duteous love
Doth cherish you and yours, God punish me
With hate in those where I expect most love!
When I have most need to employ a friend,
And most assured that he is a friend,
Deep, hollow, treacherous, and full of guile,

Be he unto me! this do I beg of God,
When I am cold in zeal to you or yours. [*They embrace.*
K. EDW. A pleasing cordial, princely Buckingham,
Is this thy vow unto my sickly heart.
There wanteth now our brother Gloucester here,
To make the perfect period of this peace.
BUCK. And, in good time, here comes the noble duke.

Enter GLOUCESTER.

GLOU. Good morrow to my sovereign king and queen;
And, princely peers, a happy time of day!
K. EDW. Happy, indeed, as we have spent the day.
Brother, we have done deeds of charity;
Made peace of enmity, fair love of hate,
Between these swelling wrong-incensed peers.
GLOU. A blessed labour, my most sovereign liege:
Amongst this princely heap, if any here,
By false intelligence, or wrong surmise,
Hold me a foe;
If I unwittingly, or in my rage,
Have aught committed that is hardly borne
By any in this presence, I desire
To reconcile me to his friendly peace:
'Tis death to me to be at enmity;
I hate it, and desire all good men's love.
First, madam, I entreat true peace of you,
Which I will purchase with my duteous service;
Of you, my noble cousin Buckingham,
If ever any grudge were lodged between us;
Of you, Lord Rivers, and, Lord Grey, of you;
That all without desert have frown'd on me;
Dukes, earls, lords, gentlemen; indeed, of all.
I do not know that Englishman alive
With whom my soul is any jot at odds

KING RICHARD III

More than the infant that is born to-night;
I thank my God for my humility.

Q. ELIZ. A holy day shall this be kept hereafter:
I would to God all strifes were well compounded.
My sovereign liege, I do beseech your majesty
To take our brother Clarence to your grace.

GLOU. Why, madam, have I offer'd love for this,
To be so flouted in this royal presence?
Who knows not that the noble duke is dead?

> [*They all start.*

You do him injury to scorn his corse.

RIV. Who knows not he is dead! who knows he is?

Q. ELIZ. All-seeing heaven, what a world is this!

BUCK. Look I so pale, Lord Dorset, as the rest?

DOR. Ay, my good lord; and no one in this presence
But his red colour hath forsook his cheeks.

K. EDW. Is Clarence dead? the order was reversed.

GLOU. But he, poor soul, by your first order died,
And that a winged Mercury did bear;
Some tardy cripple bore the countermand,
That came too lag to see him buried.
God grant that some, less noble and less loyal,
Nearer in bloody thoughts, but not in blood,
Deserve not worse than wretched Clarence did,
And yet go current from suspicion!

Enter DERBY.

DER. A boon, my sovereign, for my service done!

K. EDW. I pray thee, peace: my soul is full of sorrow.

DER. I will not rise, unless your highness grant.

K. EDW. Then speak at once what is it thou demand'st.

DER. The forfeit, sovereign, of my servant's life;
Who slew to-day a riotous gentleman
Lately attendant on the Duke of Norfolk.

THE FIRST QUEEN ELIZABETH

K. Edw. Have I tongue to doom my brother's death,
  And shall the same give pardon to a slave?
  My brother slew no man; his fault was thought,
  And yet his punishment was cruel death.
  Who sued to me for him? who, in my rage,
  Kneel'd at my feet, and bade me be advised?
  Who spake of brotherhood? who spake of love?
  Who told me how the poor soul did forsake
  The mighty Warwick, and did fight for me?
  Who told me, in the field by Tewksbury,
  When Oxford had me down, he rescued me,
  And said, 'Dear brother, live, and be a king'?
  Who told me, when we both lay in the field
  Frozen almost to death, how he did lap me
  Even in his own garments, and gave himself,
  All thin and naked, to the numb cold night?
  All this from my remembrance brutish wrath
  Sinfully pluck'd, and not a man of you
  Had so much grace to put it in my mind.
  But when your carters or your waiting-vassals
  Have done a drunken slaughter, and defaced
  The precious image of our dear Redeemer,
  You straight are on your knees for pardon, pardon;
  And I, unjustly too, must grant it you:
  But for my brother not a man would speak,
  Nor I, ungracious, speak unto myself
  For him, poor soul. The proudest of you all
  Have been beholding to him in his life;
  Yet none of you would once plead for his life.
  O God, I fear thy justice will take hold
  On me, and you, and mine, and yours for this!
  Come, Hastings, help me to my closet. Oh, poor
    Clarence!

                              [*Exeunt some with* King *and* Queen.

GLOU. This is the fruit of rashness! Mark'd you not
　How that the guilty kindred of the queen
　Look'd pale when they did hear of Clarence' death?
　O, they did urge it still unto the king!
　God will revenge it. But come, let us in,
　To comfort Edward with our company.
BUCK. We wait upon your grace.　　　　　[*exeunt.*

ACT II

SCENE II. THE PALACE

Enter the DUCHESS OF YORK, *with the two children of*
CLARENCE.

BOY. Tell me, good grandam, is our father dead?
DUCH. No, boy.
BOY. Why do you wring your hands, and beat your
　breast,
　And cry 'O Clarence, my unhappy son!'
GIRL. Why do you look on us, and shake your head,
　And call us wretches, orphans, castaways,
　If that our noble father be alive?
DUCH. My pretty cousins, you mistake me much;
　I do lament the sickness of the king,
　As loath to lose him, not your father's death;
　It were lost sorrow to wail one that's lost.
BOY. Then, grandam, you conclude that he is dead.
　The king my uncle is to blame for this:
　God will revenge it; whom I will importune
　With daily prayers all to that effect.
GIRL. And so will I.
DUCH. Peace, children, peace! the king doth love you
　well:
　Incapable and shallow innocents,
　You cannot guess who caused your father's death.

BOY. Grandam, we can; for my good uncle Gloucester
Told me, the king, provoked by the queen,
Devised impeachments to imprison him:
And when my uncle told me so, he wept,
And hugg'd me in his arm, and kindly kiss'd my cheek;
Bade me rely on him as on my father,
And he would love me dearly as his child.

DUCH. Oh, that deceit should steal such gentle shapes,
And with a virtuous vizard hide foul guile!
He is my son; yea, and therein my shame;
Yet from my dugs he drew not this deceit.

BOY. Think you my uncle did dissemble, grandam?

DUCH. Ay, boy.

BOY. I cannot think it. Hark! what noise is this?

Enter QUEEN ELIZABETH, *with her hair about her ears;*
RIVERS *and* DORSET *after her.*

Q. ELIZ. Oh, who shall hinder me to wail and weep,
To chide my fortune, and torment myself?
I'll join with black despair against my soul,
And to myself become an enemy.

DUCH. What means this scene of rude impatience?

Q. ELIZ. To make an act of tragic violence:
Edward, my lord, your son, our king, is dead.
Why grow the branches now the root is wither'd?
Why wither not the leaves the sap being gone?
If you will live, lament; if die, be brief,
That our swift-winged souls may catch the king's;
Or, like obedient subjects, follow him
To his new kingdom of perpetual rest.

DUCH. Ah, so much interest have I in thy sorrow
As I had title in thy noble husband!
I have bewept a worthy husband's death,
And lived by looking on his images:

But now two mirrors of his princely semblance
Are crack'd in pieces by malignant death,
And I for comfort have but one false glass,
Which grieves me when I see my shame in him.
Thou art a widow; yet thou art a mother,
And hast the comfort of thy children left thee:
But death hath snatch'd my husband from mine arms,
And pluck'd two crutches from my feeble limbs,
Edward and Clarence. O, what cause have I,
Thine being but a moiety of my grief,
To overgo thy plaints and drown thy cries!

BOY. Good aunt, you wept not for our father's death;
  How can we aid you with our kindred tears?

GIRL. Our fatherless distress was left unmoan'd;
  Your widow-dolour likewise be unwept!

Q. ELIZ. Give me no help in lamentation;
  I am not barren to bring forth complaints:
  All springs reduce their currents to mine eyes,
  That I, being govern'd by the watery moon,
  May send forth plenteous tears to drown the world!
  Oh for my husband, for my dear lord Edward!

CHIL. Oh for our father, for our dear lord Clarence!

DUCH. Alas for both, both mine, Edward and Clarence!

Q. ELIZ. What stay had I but Edward? and he's gone.

CHIL. What stay had we but Clarence? and he's gone.

DUCH. What stays had I but they? and they are gone.

Q. ELIZ. Was never widow had so dear a loss!

CHIL. Were never orphans had so dear a loss!

DUCH. Was never mother had so dear a loss!
  Alas, I am the mother of these moans!
  Their woes are parcell'd, mine are general.
  She for an Edward weeps, and so do I;
  I for a Clarence weep, so doth not she:
  These babes for Clarence weep, and so do I;

I for an Edward weep, so do not they:
Alas, you three, on me, threefold distress'd,
Pour all your tears! I am your sorrow's nurse,
And I will pamper it with lamentations.

DOR.   Comfort, dear mother: God is much displeased
That you take with unthankfulness his doing:
In common worldly things, 'tis call'd ungrateful,
With dull unwillingness to repay a debt
Which with a bounteous hand was kindly lent;
Much more to be thus opposite with heaven,
For it requires the royal debt it lent you.

RIV.   Madam, bethink you, like a careful mother,
Of the young prince your son; send straight for him;
Let him be crown'd; in him your comfort lives:
Drown desperate sorrow in dead Edward's grave,
And plant your joys in living Edward's throne.

Enter GLOUCESTER, BUCKINGHAM, DERBY, HASTINGS, *and*
RATCLIFF.

GLOU.   Madam, have comfort: all of us have cause
To wail the dimming of our shining star;
But none can cure their harms by wailing them.
Madam, my mother, I do cry you mercy;
I did not see your grace: humbly on my knee
I crave your blessing.

DUCH.   God bless thee; and put meekness in thy mind,
Love, charity, obedience, and true duty!

GLOU.   [*aside.*] Amen; and make me die a good old man!
That is the butt-end of a mother's blessing:
I marvel why her grace did leave it out.

BUCK.   You cloudy princes and heart-sorrowing peers,
That bear this mutual heavy load of moan,
Now cheer each other in each other's love:
Though we have spent our harvest of this king,

We are to reap the harvest of his son.
The broken rancour of your high-swoln hearts,
But lately splinter'd, knit, and join'd together,
Must gently be preserved, cherish'd, and kept:
Me seemeth good, that, with some little train,
Forthwith from Ludlow the young prince be fetch'd
Hither to London, to be crown'd our king.

RIV.   Why with some little train, my Lord of Buckingham?

BUCK.   Marry, my lord, lest, by a multitude,
The new-heal'd wound of malice should break out;
Which would be so much the more dangerous,
By how much the estate is green and yet ungovern'd:
Where every horse bears his commanding rein,
And may direct his course as please himself,
As well the fear of harm, as harm apparent,
In my opinion, ought to be prevented.

GLOU.   I hope the king made peace with all of us;
And the compact is firm and true in me.

RIV.   And so in me; and so, I think, in all:
Yet, since it is but green, it should be put
To no apparent likelihood of breach,
Which haply by much company might be urged:
Therefore I say with noble Buckingham,
That it is meet so few should fetch the prince.

HAST.   And so say I.

GLOU.   Then be it so; and go we to determine
Who they shall be that straight shall post to Ludlow.
Madam, and you, my mother, will you go
To give your censures in this weighty business?

Q. ELIZ.⎱
DUCH. ⎰   With all our hearts.

                               [Exeunt all but BUCK. *and* GLOU.

BUCK.   My lord, whoever journeys to the prince,
For God's sake, let not us two be behind;

For, by the way, I'll sort occasion,
As index to the story we late talk'd of,
To part the queen's proud kindred from the king.
GLOU. My other self, my counsel's consistory,
My oracle, my prophet! My dear cousin,
I, like a child, will go by thy direction.
Towards Ludlow then, for we'll not stay behind. [*exeunt.*

ACT II

SCENE IV. LONDON. THE PALACE

Enter the ARCHBISHOP OF YORK, *the young* DUKE OF YORK,
QUEEN ELIZABETH, *and the* DUCHESS OF YORK.

ARCH. Last night, I hear, they lay at Northampton ;
At Stony-Stratford will they be to-night :
To-morrow, or next day, they will be here.
DUCH. I long with all my heart to see the prince :
I hope he is much grown since last I saw him.
Q. ELIZ. But I hear, no ; they say my son of York
Hath almost overta'en him in his growth.
YORK. Ay, mother ; but I would not have it so.
DUCH. Why, my young cousin, it is good to grow.
YORK. Grandam, one night, as we did sit at supper,
My uncle Rivers talk'd how I did grow
More than my brother: 'Ay,' quoth my uncle Gloucester,
'Small herbs have grace, great weeds do grow apace':
And since, methinks, I would not grow so fast,
Because sweet flowers are slow and weeds make haste.
DUCH. Good faith, good faith, the saying did not hold
In him that did object the same to thee:
He was the wretched'st thing when he was young,
So long a-growing and so leisurely,
That, if this rule were true, he should be gracious.
ARCH. Why, madam, so, no doubt, he is.

DUCH. I hope he is; but yet let mothers doubt.

YORK. Now, by my troth, if I had been remember'd,
I could have given my uncle's grace a flout,
To touch his growth nearer than he touch'd mine.

DUCH. How, my pretty York? I pray thee, let me hear it.

YORK. Marry, they say my uncle grew so fast
That he could gnaw a crust at two hours old:
'Twas full two years ere I could get a tooth.
Grandam, this would have been a biting jest.

DUCH. I pray thee, pretty York, who told thee this?

YORK. Grandam, his nurse.

DUCH. His nurse! why, she was dead ere thou wert born.

YORK. If 'twere not she, I cannot tell who told me.

Q. ELIZ. A parlous boy: go to, you are too shrewd.

ARCH. Good madam, be not angry with the child.

Q. ELIZ. Pitchers have ears.

Enter a MESSENGER.

ARCH. Here comes a messenger. What news?

MESS. Such news, my lord, as grieves me to unfold.

Q. ELIZ. How fares the prince?

MESS.   Well, madam, and in health.

DUCH. What is thy news then?

MESS. Lord Rivers and Lord Grey are sent to Pomfret,
With them Sir Thomas Vaughan, prisoners.

DUCH. Who hath committed them?

MESS.   The mighty dukes
Gloucester and Buckingham.

Q. ELIZ.   For what offence?

MESS. The sum of all I can, I have disclosed;
Why or for what these nobles were committed
Is all unknown to me, my gracious lady.

Q. ELIZ. Ay me, I see the downfall of our house!
The tiger now hath seized the gentle hind;

Insulting tyranny begins to jet
Upon the innocent and aweless throne:
Welcome, destruction, death, and massacre!
I see, as in a map, the end of all.

DUCH. Accursed and unquiet wrangling days,
How many of you have mine eyes beheld!
My husband lost his life to get the crown;
And often up and down my sons were toss'd,
For me to joy and weep their gain and loss:
And being seated, and domestic broils
Clean over-blown, themselves, the conquerors,
Make war upon themselves; blood against blood,
Self against self: O, preposterous
And frantic outrage, end thy damned spleen;
Or let me die, to look on death no more!

Q. ELIZ. Come, come, my boy; we will to sanctuary.
Madam farewell.

DUCH.   I'll go along with you.

Q. ELIZ. You have no cause.

ARCH.   My gracious lady, go;
And thither bear your treasure and your goods.
For my part, I'll resign unto your grace
The seal I keep; and so betide to me
As well I tender you and all of yours!
Come, I'll conduct you to the sanctuary.   [*exeunt.*

ACT IV

SCENE I. BEFORE THE TOWER

Enter, on one side, QUEEN ELIZABETH, DUCHESS OF YORK,
and MARQUESS OF DORSET ; *on the other,* ANNE,
DUCHESS OF GLOUCESTER, *leading* LADY MARGARET
PLANTAGENET, CLARENCE'S *young Daughter.*

DUCH. Who meets us here? my niece Plantagenet

Led in the hand of her kind aunt of Gloucester?
Now, for my life, she's wandering to the Tower,
On pure heart's love to greet the tender princes.
Daughter, well met.

ANNE.   God give your graces both
A happy and a joyful time of day!

Q. ELIZ. As much to you good sister! Wither away?

ANNE. No farther than the Tower; and, as I guess,
Upon the like devotion as yourselves,
To gratulate the gentle princes there.

Q. ELIZ. Kind sister, thanks: we'll enter all together.

Enter BRAKENBURY.

And in good time, here the lieutenant comes.
Master lieutenant, pray you, by your leave,
How doth the prince, and my young son of York?

BRAK. Right well, dear madam. By your patience,
I may not suffer you to visit them;
The king hath straitly charged the contrary.

Q. ELIZ. The king! why, who's that?

BRAK. I cry you mercy: I mean the lord protector.

Q. ELIZ. The Lord protect him from that kingly title!
Hath he set bounds betwixt their love and me?
I am their mother; who should keep me from them?

DUCH. I am their father's mother; I will see them.

ANNE. Their aunt I am in law, in love their mother:
Then bring me to their sights; I'll bear thy blame
And take thy office from thee, on my peril.

BRAK. No, madam, no: I may not leave it so:
I am bound by oath, and therefore pardon me.   [*exit.*

Enter LORD STANLEY.

STAN. Let me but meet you, ladies, one hour hence,
And I'll salute your grace of York as mother,

THE FIRST QUEEN ELIZABETH

And reverend looker on, of two fair queens.
[*to* ANNE.]   Come, madam, you must straight to Westminster,
There to be crowned Richard's royal queen.

Q. ELIZ.   O, cut my lace in sunder, that my pent heart
May have some scope to beat, or else I swoon
With this dead-killing news!

ANNE.   Despiteful tidings! O unpleasing news!

DOR.   Be of good cheer: mother, how fares your grace?

Q. ELIZ.   O Dorset, speak not to me, get thee hence!
Death and destruction dog thee at the heels;
Thy mother's name is ominous to children.
If thou wilt outstrip death, go across the seas,
And live with Richmond, from the reach of hell:
Go, hie thee, hie thee from this slaughter-house,
Lest thou increase the number of the dead;
And make me die the thrall of Margaret's curse,
Nor mother, wife, nor England's counted queen.

STAN.   Full of wise care is this your counsel, madam.
Take all the swift advantage of the hours;
You shall have letters from me to my son
To meet you on the way, and welcome you.
Be not ta'en tardy by unwise delay.

DUCH.   O ill-dispersing wind of misery!
O my accursed womb, the bed of death!
A cockatrice hast thou hatch'd to the world,
Whose unavoided eye is murderous.

STAN.   Come, madam, come; I in all haste was sent.

ANNE.   And I in all unwillingness will go.
I would to God that the inclusive verge
Of golden metal that must round my brow
Were red-hot steel, to sear me to the brain!
Anointed let me be with deadly venom,
And die, ere men can say, God save the Queen!

278

Q. ELIZ.   Go, go, poor soul, I envy not thy glory;
  To feed my humour, wish thyself no harm.
ANNE.   No! why?   When he that is my husband now
  Came to me, as I follow'd Henry's corse,
  When scarce the blood was well wash'd from his hands
  Which issued from my other angel husband
  And that dead saint which then I weeping follow'd;
  O, when, I say, I look'd on Richard's face,
  This was my wish: 'Be thou,' quoth I, 'accursed,
  For making me, so young, so old a widow!
  And, when thou wed'st, let sorrow haunt thy bed;
  And be thy wife—if any be so mad—
  As miserable by the life of thee
  As thou hast made me by my dear lord's death!'
  Lo, ere I can repeat this curse again,
  Even in so short a space, my woman's heart
  Grossly grew captive to his honey words
  And proved the subject of my own soul's curse,
  Which ever since hath kept my eyes from rest;
  For never yet one hour in his bed
  Have I enjoy'd the golden dew of sleep,
  But have been waked by his timorous dreams.
  Besides, he hates me for my father Warwick;
  And will, no doubt, shortly be rid of me.
Q. ELIZ.   Poor heart, adieu! I pity thy complaining.
ANNE.   No more than from my soul I mourn for yours.
Q. ELIZ.   Farewell, thou woful welcomer of glory!
ANNE.   Adieu, poor soul, that takest thy leave of it!
DUCH.   [to DORSET.] Go thou to Richmond, and good
  fortune guide thee!
  [to ANNE.] Go thou to Richard, and good angels guard
  thee!
  [to QUEEN ELIZ.]   Go thou to sanctuary, and good
  thoughts possess thee!

I to my grave, where peace and rest lie with me!
Eighty odd years of sorrow have I seen,
And each hour's joy wreck'd with a week of teen.
Q. ELIZ.   Stay, yet look back with me unto the Tower.
Pity, you ancient stones, those tender babes
Whom envy hath immured within your walls!
Rough cradle for such little pretty ones!
Rude ragged nurse, old sullen playfellow
For tender princes, use my babies well!
So foolish sorrow bids your stones farewell.

ACT IV

SCENE IV.   BEFORE THE PALACE

Enter QUEEN MARGARET.

Q. MAR.   So, now prosperity begins to mellow
And drop into the rotten mouth of death.
Here in these confines slily have I lurk'd,
To watch the waning of mine adversaries. . . .

Enter QUEEN ELIZABETH *and the* DUCHESS OF YORK.

Q. ELIZ.   Ah, my young princes! ah, my tender babes!
My unblown flowers, new-appearing sweets!
If yet your gentle souls fly in the air
And be not fixed in doom perpetual,
Hover about me with your airy wings
And hear your mother's lamentation!
Q. MAR.   Hover about her; say, that right for right
Hath dimm'd your infant morn to aged night.
DUCH.   So many miseries have crazed my voice,
That my woe-wearied tongue is mute and dumb.
Edward Plantagenet, why art thou dead?
Q. MAR.   Plantagenet doth quit Plantagenet.
Edward for Edward pays a dying debt.

Q. Eliz.   Wilt thou, O God, fly from such gentle lambs,
   And throw them in the entrails of the wolf?
   When didst thou sleep when such a deed was done?
Q. Mar.   When holy Harry died, and my sweet son.
Duch.   Blind sight, dead life, poor mortal living ghost,
   Woe's scene, world's shame, grave's due by life usurp'd,
   Brief abstract and record of tedious days,
   Rest thy unrest on England's lawful earth,   [*sitting down.*
   Unlawfully made drunk with innocents' blood!
Q. Eliz.   O, that thou wouldst as well afford a grave
   As thou canst yield a melancholy seat!
   Then would I hide my bones, not rest them here.
   O, who hath any cause to mourn but I?
Q. Mar.   If ancient sorrow be most reverend,
   Give mine the benefit of seniory,
   And let my woes frown on the upper hand.

.   .   .   .   .

Q. Eliz.   O thou well skill'd in curses, stay awhile,
   And teach me how to curse mine enemies!
Q. Mar.   Forbear to sleep the nights, and fast the days;
   Compare dead happiness with living woe;
   Think that thy babes were fairer than they were,
   And he that slew them fouler than he is:
   Bettering thy loss makes the bad causer worse:
   Revolving this will teach thee how to curse.
Q. Eliz.   My words are dull; O, quicken them with thine!
Q. Mar.   Thy woes will make them sharp, and pierce
      like mine.   [*exit.*
Duch.   Why should calamity be full of words?
Q. Eliz.   Windy attorneys to their client woes,
   Airy succeeders of intestate joys,
   Poor breathing orators of miseries!
   Let them have scope; though what they do impart
   Help not at all, yet do they ease the heart.
Duch.   If so, then be not tongue-tied: go with me,

And in the breath of bitter words let's smother
My damned son, which thy two sweet sons smothered.
I hear his drum: be copious in exclaims.

Enter KING RICHARD, *marching, with drums and trumpets.*

K. RICH. Who intercepts my expedition?
DUCH. O, she that might have intercepted thee,
  By strangling thee in her accursed womb,
  From all the slaughters, wretch, that thou hast done!
Q. ELIZ. Hidest thou that forehead with a golden crown,
  Where should be graven, if that right were right,
  The slaughter of the prince that owed that crown,
  And the dire death of my two sons and brothers?
  Tell me, thou villain slave, where are my children?
DUCH. Thou toad, thou toad, where is thy brother Clarence?
  And little Ned Plantagenet, his son?
Q. ELIZ. Where is kind Hastings, Rivers, Vaughan, Grey?
K. RICH. A flourish, trumpets! strike alarum, drums!
  Let not the heavens hear these tell-tale women
  Rail on the Lord's anointed: strike, I say! [*Flourish. Alarums.*
  Either be patient, and entreat me fair,
  Or with the clamorous report of war
  Thus will I drown your exclamations. . . .
DUCH. Art thou so hasty? I have stay'd for thee,
  God knows, in anguish, pain and agony.
K. RICH. And came I not at last to comfort you?
DUCH. No, by the holy rood, thou know'st it well.
  Thou camest on earth to make the earth my hell.
  A grievous burthen was thy birth to me;
  Tetchy and wayward was thy infancy;
  Thy school-days frightful, desperate, wild and furious,
  Thy prime of manhood daring, bold, and venturous,
  Thy age confirm'd, proud, subtle, bloody, treacherous,
  More mild, but yet more harmful, kind in hatred:

What comfortable hour canst thou name,
That ever graced me in thy company?

K. RICH.   Faith, none, but Humphrey Hour, that call'd
  your grace
To breakfast once forth of my company.
If I be so disgracious in your sight,
Let me march on, and not offend your grace.
Strike up the drum.

DUCH.   I prithee, hear me speak.

K. RICH.   You speak too bitterly.

DUCH.   Hear me a word;
For I shall never speak to thee again.

K. RICH.   So.

DUCH.   Either thou wilt die, by God's just ordinance,
Ere from this war thou turn a conqueror,
Or I with grief and extreme age shall perish
And never look upon thy face again.
Therefore take with thee my most heavy curse;
Which, in the day of battle, tire thee more
Than all the complete armour that thou wear'st!
My prayers on the adverse party fight;
And there the little souls of Edward's children
Whisper the spirits of thine enemies
And promise them success and victory.
Bloody thou art, bloody will be thy end,
Shame serves thy life and doth thy death attend. [*exit.*

Q. ELIZ.   Though far more cause, yet much less spirit
  to curse
Abides in me; I say amen to all.

K. RICH.   Stay, madam; I must speak a word with you.

Q. ELIZ.   I have no moe sons of the royal blood
For thee to murder: for my daughters, Richard,
They shall be praying nuns, not weeping queens;
And therefore level not to hit their lives.

K. RICH. You have a daughter call'd Elizabeth,
  Virtuous and fair, royal and gracious.
Q. ELIZ. And must she die for this? O let her live,
  And I'll corrupt her manners, stain her beauty;
  Slander myself as false to Edward's bed;
  Throw over her the veil of infamy:
  So she may live unscarr'd of bleeding slaughter,
  I will confess she was not Edward's daughter.
K. RICH. Wrong not her birth, she is of royal blood.
Q. ELIZ. To save her life, I'll say she is not so.
K. RICH. Her life is only safest in her birth.
Q. ELIZ. And only in that safety died her brothers.
K. RICH. Lo, at their birth good stars were opposite.
Q. ELIZ. No, to their lives bad friends were contrary.
K. RICH. All unavoided is the doom of destiny.
Q. ELIZ. True, when avoided grace makes destiny:
  My babes were destined to a fairer death,
  If grace had bless'd thee with a fairer life.
K. RICH. You speak as if that I had slain my cousins.
Q. ELIZ. Cousins, indeed; and by their uncle cozen'd
  Of comfort, kingdom, kindred, freedom, life.
  Whose hand soever lanced their tender hearts,
  Thy head, all indirectly, gave direction:
  No doubt the murderous knife was dull and blunt
  Till it was whetted on thy stone-hard heart,
  To revel in the entrails of my lambs.
  But that still use of grief makes wild grief tame,
  My tongue should to thy ears not name my boys
  Till that my nails were anchor'd in thine eyes;
  And I, in such a desperate bay of death,
  Like a poor bark, of sails and tackling reft,
  Rush all to pieces on thy rocky bosom.
K. RICH. Madam, so thrive I in my enterprise
  And dangerous success of bloody wars,

As I intend more good to you and yours
Than ever you or yours were by me wrong'd!

Q. ELIZ. What good is cover'd with the face of heaven,
To be discover'd, that can do me good?

K. RICH. The advancement of your children, gentle lady.

Q. ELIZ. Up to some scaffold, there to lose their heads?

K. RICH. No, to the dignity and height of honour,
The high imperial type of this earth's glory.

Q. ELIZ. Flatter my sorrows with report of it;
Tell me what state, what dignity, what honour,
Canst thou demise to any child of mine?

K. RICH. Even all I have; yea, and myself and all,
Will I withal endow a child of thine;
So in the Lethe of thy angry soul
Thou drown the sad remembrance of those wrongs
Which thou supposest I have done to thee.

Q. ELIZ. Be brief, lest that the process of thy kindness
Last longer telling than thy kindness' date.

K. RICH. Then know, that from my soul I love thy daughter.

Q. ELIZ. My daughter's mother thinks it with her soul.

K. RICH. What do you think?

Q. ELIZ. That thou dost love my daughter from thy soul:
So from thy soul's love didst thou love her brothers;
And from my heart's love I do thank thee for it.

K. RICH. Be not so hasty to confound my meaning:
I mean, that with my soul I love thy daughter.
And mean to make her queen of England.

Q. ELIZ. Say then, who dost thou mean shall be her king?

K. RICH. Even he that makes her queen: who should be else?

Q. ELIZ. What, thou?

K. RICH. I, even I: what think you of it, madam?

Q. ELIZ. How canst thou woo her?

K. RICH.   That would I learn of you,
As one that are best acquainted with her humour.

Q. ELIZ.   And wilt thou learn of me?

K. RICH.   Madam, with all my heart.

Q. ELIZ. Send to her, by the man that slew her brothers,
A pair of bleeding hearts; thereon engrave
Edward and York; then haply she will weep:
Therefore present to her,—as sometime Margaret
Did to thy father, steep'd in Rutland's blood,—
A handkerchief; which, say to her, did drain
The purple sap from her sweet brother's body.
And bid her dry her weeping eyes therewith.
If this inducement force her not to love,
Send her a story of thy noble acts;
Tell her thou madest away her uncle Clarence,
Her uncle Rivers; yea, and, for her sake,
Madest quick conveyance with her good aunt Anne.

K. RICH.   Come, come, you mock me; this is not the way
To win your daughter.

Q. ELIZ.   There is no other way;
Unless thou couldst put on some other shape,
And not be Richard that hath done all this.

K. RICH.   Say that I did all this for love of her.

Q.ELIZ.   Nay, then indeed she cannot choose but hate thee,
Having bought love with such a bloody spoil.

K. RICH.   Look, what is done cannot be now amended:
Men shall deal unadvisedly sometimes,
Which after hours give leisure to repent.
If I did take the kingdom from your sons,
To make amends, I'll give it to your daughter.
If I have kill'd the issue of your womb,
To quicken your increase, I will beget
Mine issue of your blood upon your daughter:
A grandam's name is little less in love
Than is the doting title of a mother;
They are as children but one step below,
Even of your mettle, of your very blood;

Of all one pain, save for a night of groans
Endured of her, for whom you bid like sorrow.
Your children were vexation to your youth,
But mine shall be a comfort to your age.
The loss you have is but a son being king,
And by that loss your daughter is made queen.
I cannot make you what amends I would,
Therefore accept such kindness as I can.
Dorset your son, that with a fearful soul
Leads discontented steps in foreign soil,
This fair alliance quickly shall call home
To high promotions and great dignity:
The king, that calls your beauteous daughter wife,
Familiarly shall call thy Dorset brother;
Again shall you be mother to a king,
And all the ruins of distressful times
Repair'd with double riches of content.
What! we have many goodly days to see:
The liquid drops of tears that you have shed
Shall come again, transform'd to orient pearl,
Advantaging their loan with interest
Of ten times double gain of happiness.
Go, then, my mother, to thy daughter go;
Make bold her bashful years with your experience;
Prepare her ears to hear a wooer's tale;
Put in her tender heart the aspiring flame
Of golden sovereignty; acquaint the princess
With the sweet silent hours of marriage joys:
And when this arm of mine hath chastised
The petty rebel, dull-brain'd Buckingham,
Bound with triumphant garlands will I come
And lead thy daughter to a conqueror's bed;
To whom I will retail my conquest won,
And she shall be sole victress, Cæsar's Cæsar.

Q. ELIZ.   What were I best to say? her father's brother

Would be her lord? or shall I say, her uncle?
Or, he that slew her brothers and her uncles?
Under what title shall I woo for thee,
That God, the law, my honour and her love,
Can make seem pleasing to her tender years?

K. RICH. Infer fair England's peace by this alliance.

Q. ELIZ. Which she shall purchase with still lasting war.

K. RICH. Say that the king, which may command, entreats.

Q. ELIZ. That at her hands which the king's King forbids.

K. RICH. Say, she shall be a high and mighty queen.

Q. ELIZ. To wail the title as her mother doth.

K. RICH. Say, I will love her everlastingly.

Q. ELIZ. But how long shall that title 'ever' last?

K. RICH. Sweetly in force unto her fair life's end.

Q. ELIZ. But how long fairly shall her sweet life last?

K. RICH. So long as heaven and nature lengthens it.

Q. ELIZ. So long as hell and Richard likes of it.

K. RICH. Say, I, her sovereign, am her subject love.

Q. ELIZ. But she, your subject, loathes such sovereignty.

K. RICH. Be eloquent in my behalf to her.

Q. ELIZ. An honest tale speeds best being plainly told.

K. RICH. Then in plain terms tell her my loving tale.

Q. ELIZ. Plain and not honest is too harsh a style.

K. RICH. Your reasons are too shallow and too quick.

Q. ELIZ. O no, my reasons are too deep and dead;
Too deep and dead, poor infants, in their grave.

K. RICH. Harp not on that string, madam; that is past.

Q. ELIZ. Harp on it still shall I till heart-strings break.

K. RICH. Now, by my George, my garter, and my crown,—

Q. ELIZ. Profaned, dishonour'd, and the third usurp'd.

K. RICH. I swear—

Q. ELIZ.   By nothing; for this is no oath:
The George, profaned, hath lost his holy honour;
The garter, blemish'd, pawn'd his knightly virtue;

The crown, usurp'd, disgraced his kingly glory.
If something thou wilt swear to be believed,
Swear then by something that thou hast not wrong'd.

K. RICH. Now, by the world—

Q. ELIZ.   'Tis full of thy foul wrongs.

K. RICH. My father's death—

Q. ELIZ.   Thy life hath that dishonour'd.

K. RICH. Then, by myself—

Q. ELIZ.   Thyself thyself misusest.

K. RICH. Why then, by God—

Q. ELIZ.   God's wrong is most of all.
If thou hadst fear'd to break an oath by Him,
The unity the king thy brother made
Had not been broken, nor my brother slain:
If thou hadst fear'd to break an oath by Him,
The imperial metal, circling now thy brow,
Had graced the tender temples of my child,
And both the princes had been breathing here,
Which now, two slender playfellows for dust,
Thy broken faith hath made a prey for worms.
What canst thou swear by now?

K. RICH.   The time to come.

Q. ELIZ. That thou hast wronged in the time o'erpast;
For I myself have many tears to wash
Hereafter time, for time past wrong'd by thee.
The children live, whose parents thou hast slaughter'd,
Ungovern'd youth, to wail it in their age;
The parents live, whose children thou hast butcher'd,
Old wither'd plants, to wail it with their age.
Swear not by time to come; for that thou hast
Misused ere used, by time misused o'erpast.

K. RICH. As I intend to prosper and repent,
So thrive I in my dangerous attempt

289

Of hostile arms! myself myself confound!
Heaven and fortune bar me happy hours!
Day, yield me not thy light; nor, night, thy rest!
Be opposite all planets of good luck
To my proceedings, if, with pure heart's love,
Immaculate devotion, holy thoughts,
I tender not thy beauteous princely daughter!
In her consists my happiness and thine;
Without her, follows to this land and me,
To thee, herself, and many a Christian soul,
Death, desolation, ruin and decay:
It cannot be avoided but by this;
It will not be avoided but by this.
Therefore, good mother,—I must call you so—
Be the attorney of my love to her:
Plead what I will be, not what I have been;
Not my deserts, but what I will deserve:
Urge the necessity and state of times,
And be not peevish-fond in great designs.

Q. ELIZ.   Shall I be tempted of the devil thus?
K. RICH.   Ay, if the devil tempt thee to do good.
Q. ELIZ.   Shall I forget myself to be myself?
K. RICH.   Ay, if yourself's remembrance wrong yourself.
Q. ELIZ.   But thou didst kill my children.
K. RICH.   But in your daughter's womb I bury them:
Where in that nest of spicery they shall breed
Selves of themselves, to your recomforture.
Q. ELIZ.   Shall I go win my daughter to thy will?
K. RICH.   And be a happy mother by the deed.
Q. ELIZ.   I go. Write to me very shortly,
And you shall understand from me her mind.
K. RICH.   Bear her my true love's kiss; and so, farewell.

[*exit* QUEEN ELIZABETH.

Relenting fool, and shallow, changing woman!

BIBLIOGRAPHY

Archæologia, vol. 26. Society of Antiquaries. (London, 1836.)

Calendar of State Papers and Manuscripts existing in the Archives and Collections of Milan, vol. i. Edited A. B. Hinds. (London, 1912).

Chronicle of London. Edited by Sir H. Nicolas. (London, 1827.)

Chronicles of the White Rose of York. (Bohn, 1845.)

Collections of Ordinances and Regulations for the Government of the Royal Household. (London, 1790.)

COMMINES, PHILIPPE DE: *Mémoires*, ed. Dupont. (Paris, 1840.)

DAVIES: *English Chronicle.* (Camden Society, 1856.)

ELLIS, HENRY: *Original Letters*, Series 2, vol. i. (London, 1827.)

Excerpta Historica. Nicolas. (London, 1831.)

FABYAN, ROBERT: *The New Chronicles of England and France.* Ed. Ellis. (London, 1811.)

Friends of Canterbury Cathedral. Tenth Annual Report. Article by M. A. S. Hickmore. (1937.)

GRAY, J. H.: *History of the Queens' College, Cambridge.* (Cambridge, 1926.)

GREEN, M. A. E.: *Lives of the Princesses of England.* (London, 1849.)

HALL, EDWARD: *Chronicle.* (Ellis. London, 1809.)

GAIRDNER, James: *Life and Reign of Richard III.* (London, 1879.)

ditto. *Lancaster and York.* (London, 1875.)

Liber Niger Scaccarii. T. Hearne. (Oxford, 1728.)

MORE, THOMAS: *The History of Richard III.* Ed. J. R. Lumby. (Cambridge, 1883.)

OMAN, Sir CHARLES: *Warwick the Kingmaker.* (London, 1893.)

Paston Letters. Ed. James Gairdner. (Westminster, 1900.)

RAMSEY, Sir J. H.: *Lancaster and York*, vol. ii. (Oxford, 1892.)

RYMER, THOMAS: *Foedera, etc.*, vols. xi and xii. (London, 1709.)

SANDFORD, F.: *Genealogical History of the Kings and Queens of England.* (1707.)

THE FIRST QUEEN ELIZABETH

SCOFIELD, CORA L.: *The Life and Reign of Edward the Fourth.* (Longmans, 1923.)

SMITH, GEORGE: *The Coronation of Elizabeth Wydeville.* (Ellis, 1935.)

STRATFORD, LAURENCE: *Edward the Fourth.* (Pitman, 1910.)

STRICKLAND, AGNES: *Lives of the Queens of England.* (London, 1864.)

TEMPERLEY, GLADYS: *Henry VII.* (Constable, 1914.)

WOOD, M. A. E.: *Letters of Royal and Illustrious Ladies of Great Britain.* (London, 1846.)

Wardrobe Accounts of Edward IV. Nicolas. (London, 1830.)

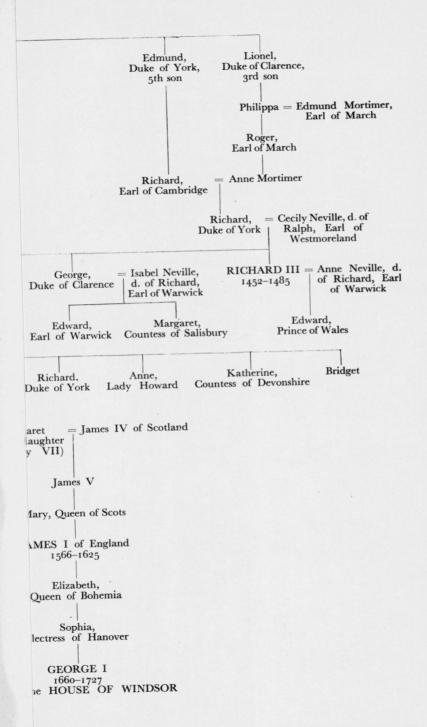

Edmund,
Duke of York,
5th son

Lionel,
Duke of Clarence,
3rd son

Philippa = Edmund Mortimer,
Earl of March

Roger,
Earl of March

Richard, = Anne Mortimer
Earl of Cambridge

Richard, = Cecily Neville, d. of
Duke of York | Ralph, Earl of
Westmoreland

George, = Isabel Neville,
Duke of Clarence | d. of Richard,
Earl of Warwick

RICHARD III = Anne Neville, d.
1452–1485 | of Richard, Earl
of Warwick

Edward,
Earl of Warwick

Margaret,
Countess of Salisbury

Edward,
Prince of Wales

Richard,
Duke of York

Anne,
Lady Howard

Katherine,
Countess of Devonshire

Bridget

aret = James IV of Scotland
laughter
y VII)

James V

Mary, Queen of Scots

JAMES I of England
1566–1625

Elizabeth,
Queen of Bohemia

Sophia,
lectress of Hanover

GEORGE I
1660–1727
he HOUSE OF WINDSOR

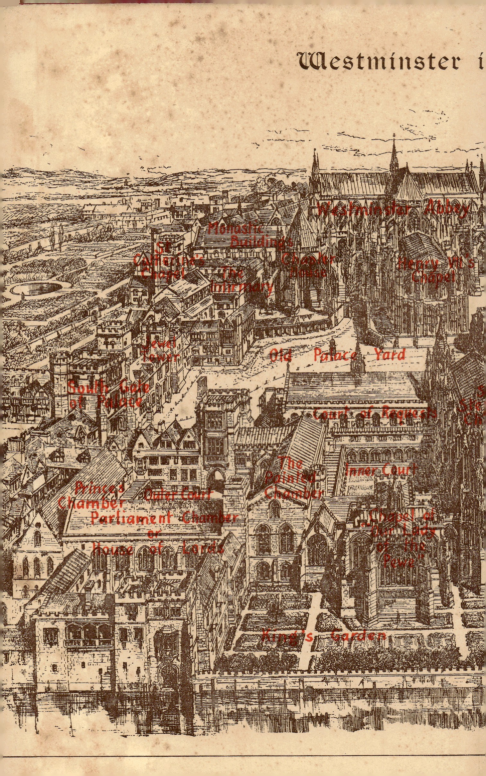

Westminster i